PRAYING THROUGH THE NAMES OF JESUS

TONY EVANS

HARVEST HOUSE PUBLISHERS
EUGENE, OREGON

Cover design by Bryce Williamson

Cover photos © Pearl / Lightstock ; yukipon / Getty Images

The prayers in this book were inspired by Dr. Evans' teaching but were written with the help of his writing assistant, Heather Hair.

Praying Through the Names of Jesus
Copyright © 2019 by Tony Evans
Published by Harvest House Publishers
Eugene, Oregon 97408
www.harvesthousepublishers.com

ISBN 978-0-7369-7530-8 (pbk.)
ISBN 978-0-7369-7531-5 (eBook)

Library of Congress Cataloging-in-Publication Data is on file at the Library of Congress, Washington, DC.

Printed in the United States of America
19 20 21 22 23 24 25 26 27 / BP-GL / 10 9 8 7 6 5 4 3 2 1

CONTENTS

INTRODUCTION

The power of Jesus' names exists in many forms. His love, might, strength, mercy, forgiveness, grace, rule, and multiple other expressions of who He is show up in the many names by which He is known. Jesus has formal names which we are all familiar with, such as Immanuel, Messiah, and Lord. He also has informal names which we call on when we are in need, such as the branch of the Lord, kinsman redeemer, or rose of Sharon. Whatever your need, Jesus has a name for it. This is because all that is needed for you to live your life to the fullest is found in Him (John 10:10). He is your rescuer, redeemer, counselor, and friend.

In this book I have provided guided prayers for you to use as you call on the various names of Jesus. To call on one of His names is to call on the character and attributes which that particular name represents. As you go through this book, I hope you will come to know many of the names of Jesus like you have never known them before. There is power in His names. As you learn to align your life under His names, you will tap into His power.

There are numerous names of Jesus in Scripture. Each one relates to an expression of who He is and how He relates to you. As you pray based on His names, you seek Him based on the revelation of each particular name. You will get to know Him better as a result.

To help facilitate your communication with Jesus based on His many names, I have provided four prayers for each of the names featured in this book. Prayer is earthly permission for heavenly interference. Prayer is communication with God. God longs to be involved with you on a very personal level. Prayer opens the door for this to happen. I want to encourage you to pray regularly, as abiding in Jesus is one of the most important things you can do in life. You can use the guided prayers word for word, or you can use them as a springboard to your own prayers directed toward the attributes of each specific name of Jesus. Or you can pray a combination of these. It doesn't matter. What matters is that you pray.

The recorded prayers in this book are based on the prayer acronym ACTS: Adoration, Confession, Thanksgiving, and Supplication. This acronym is not a magic formula. Rather, it is a structure wherein our prayers can cover important aspects of communication with God.

I also want you to use this book to help you focus more intently on your abiding relationship with Jesus. As you do so, you can follow this helpful outline to nurture your time with the Lord:

- **Identify** a time when you can focus on Jesus each day. In the book of John, this is called "abiding."
- **Consider** several ways to nurture your relationship with Jesus during this time. For example, you could write in a journal any thoughts you have toward Him or thank Him for any of His attributes. Or you could look up Scripture about Jesus and meditate on it for a few minutes.
- **Evaluate** how your relationship deepens as you spend consistent time with Immanuel ("God with us"). Also evaluate whether or not it becomes easier to proclaim Jesus through your words and actions the more you abide in Him.
- **Repeat.** After you've put this practice into play for a week, seek to repeat it in the weeks to come. You can incorporate

the various prayers in this book into your daily intimate time with Him.

Jesus is the comprehensive statement, reflection, and manifestation of God. He is sufficient for all of life. But I don't want you to misunderstand and assume that fixing your eyes on Jesus means you won't have any challenges. No, it doesn't mean you won't have any problems. But it does mean that the crucifixion of Friday will become the resurrection of Sunday in your own life.

Knowing and praying through Jesus' names will bring stability and strength in areas such as your emotional well-being, personal development, relational needs, living out your purpose, understanding grace, and overcoming temptation. May God use this book to encourage and assist you in your communication with our Lord and Savior Jesus Christ!

1

JESUS

She will bear a Son; and you shall call His name Jesus,
for He will save His people from their sins.

MATTHEW 1:21

Adoration

Jesus, the name above all names. Jesus, the name that means Savior, rescuer, and deliverer. You are all of these things and more. When You were named as a baby, Jesus was a fairly common name in that time period. But it is not common anymore. You have made this name untouchable. You have made this name unique. This is the name that embodies power. When the name Jesus is connected to Your will and authority, nothing is impossible to accomplish. I worship You, Jesus. I bow before You, Jesus. I honor You, Jesus, with all my heart, mind, and soul.

Confession

Jesus, I confess that at times I take Your name in vain or treat it lightly. I use it without the reverence that Your name deserves. Maybe I simply tag it onto the end of a prayer or call it out during a surprised moment in a conversation. Whatever the case, it is not held in the esteem and honor that Your life, death, and sacrifice deserve. I am sorry for that, and I ask that You please forgive me and cleanse my mind from such superfluous uses of Your name. Let me cherish and treasure Your many names as they should be cherished and treasured.

Thanksgiving

Thank You, Jesus, for honoring me with Your presence. Thank You for honoring humanity with Your life. Thank You for allowing us a glimpse of God and a peek into eternity. Your willingness to take on flesh, bone, and sinew in order to live on earth as the God-man, Jesus, taught us humans so much during that time and continues to teach us as we are able to learn of Your ways and read the words You said as recorded by others. Thank You for familiarizing the divine in choosing this common name, Jesus, and a less-than-common birthplace, a stable. In this way, You have made Yourself approachable. Thank You for creating the way for me to know You more fully through Your time on earth.

Supplication

Jesus, I pray that You will help me live in the level of humility that You did. You are God. You created the universe. Your infinite wisdom and knowledge reach beyond the stars. Yet You humbled Yourself and came in the form of a man, as Jesus. You ate, became hungry, slept, walked, and got tired. You laughed, cried, and probably got bored. Help me not seek to be so "spiritual" that I become irrelevant to the culture around me. Help me not become so heavenly minded that I wind up being no earthly good, as the saying goes. Help me love like You, Jesus, in every expression of love which exists.

2

LAMB

All who dwell on the earth will worship him,
everyone whose name has not been written
from the foundation of the world in the book of life
of the Lamb who has been slain.

<small>REVELATION 13:8</small>

Adoration

Jesus, You are the Lamb who has been slain. Through Your sacrificial atonement, I have received full acceptance from God. I adore You for who You are. I worship You for who You are. I marvel at You for being able and willing to humble Yourself to such a degree that You would offer Yourself as a Lamb for our salvation. As 1 Peter 1:19 states, You are without blemish and without defect—"precious blood, as of a lamb unblemished and spotless, the blood of Christ." You are sinless and perfect.

Confession

Jesus, I confess that I am in need of Your sacrifice. I bring my sins to You, the pure and faultless Lamb, because my sins are many. I share in the emotion of John the Baptist, who declared to everyone around him that one was coming to remove the punishment for sin. In John

1:29 he shouted, "Behold, the Lamb of God who takes away the sin of the world!" I come to You with my sin, asking You to take it away along with the consequences of my wrong choices.

Thanksgiving

Jesus, I thank You for Your cleansing power and the gift of grace given to me through Your shed blood. I am grateful for the forgiveness of my sins and that, as Romans 8:1 says, "There is now no condemnation for those who are in Christ Jesus." It is only through the blood of the Lamb—through You, Jesus—that I can live each day without condemnation. Thank You for ridding me of shame, guilt, and fear of punishment. I love You.

Supplication

Jesus, I ask that You help me live with a greater level of confidence in this name of Yours. Reduce my fears and worries concerning my own past failures and present bondage. Let me bask in Your light now as a reflection of Your light which will one day shine in eternity. As it says in Revelation 21:23, "The city has no need of the sun or of the moon to shine on it, for the glory of God has illumined it, and its lamp is the Lamb." Let me experience You in such a way that Your light guides me in the paths I should take. I ask for Your radiant light to shine over all I do as I rest in the forgiving power in this name, Jesus the Lamb of God.

3

HEIR OF ALL THINGS

God, after He spoke long ago to the
fathers in the prophets in many
portions and in many ways,
in these last days has spoken to us in His Son,
whom He appointed heir of all things,
through whom also He made the world.

HEBREWS 1:1-2

Adoration

Jesus, I adore You and honor You as the heir of all things. You have been named the rightful heir of all rule, power, authority, and dominion. At Your word, it is done. As the centurion honored You in his faith, I want to do the same. It is written that You marveled at the level of faith he had in You, as he knew that You had a rightful claim to command whatever You wanted on earth. As Scripture tells me in Matthew 8:8-9, "The centurion said, 'Lord, I am not worthy for You to come under my roof, but just say the word, and my servant will be healed. For I also am a man under authority, with soldiers under me; and I say to this one, "Go!" and he goes, and to another, "Come!" and he comes, and to my slave, "Do this!" and he does it.'" Jesus, heir of all things, I want You to marvel at my

faith in You as well. Let me begin by praising You for Your ownership and command of all.

Confession

Jesus, I confess to You that I become far more excited about the
rule and power and blessing provided to *me* through Your reigning
as heir of all things. And yet while You graciously give me this and
more through Your sacrifice, causing me to be a joint heir in You, You
also ask me to align myself in and with You entirely. This includes
aligning myself with Your suffering. As Romans 8:16-17 states, "The
Spirit Himself testifies with our spirit that we are children of God,
and if children, heirs also, heirs of God and fellow heirs with Christ,
if indeed we suffer with Him so that we may also be glorified with
Him." The glory comes after the suffering. I confess I often seek
the glory—or complain when I don't get it—without the suffering.
Please forgive me.

Thanksgiving

Jesus, thank You that You are an heir who shares. You are full of
love, grace, and mercy. It is because of You that I am also an heir and
recipient of God's promises and provision. I am encouraged by Titus
3:7, which reminds me "that being justified by His grace we would
be made heirs according to the hope of eternal life." Not only did
You justify me as the Lamb of God through Your sacrifice, but Your
authority as heir of all things has named me an heir, as well, according to the hope found in You. Thank You for lifting me above my circumstances and station in life.

Supplication

Jesus, as heir of all things, I know that You provide access to all I
need through my abiding relationship with You. I ask that You keep
my mind focused on You. It is easy to get so distracted by life itself

that You become a figurine on a shelf or an item to mark off my list. I am foolish to marginalize You in this way. Please help me deepen my intimacy with You. Help me discover what brings You joy and how to maintain regular fellowship and communication with You.

4

Good Shepherd

*I am the good shepherd; the good shepherd
lays down His life for the sheep.*

Adoration

Jesus, You are my good shepherd. I lift up Your name in praise and adoration. You have humbled Yourself from the throne that is rightfully Yours in order to guide me, restore me, and protect me. Why You would leave the comforts of Your glory in order to serve as my good shepherd is beyond my understanding. But I worship You for it. I worship You for Your willingness to dirty Your hands while cleaning me up. I worship You for Your ability to steer me in the right direction despite the many times I wander off. I honor Your commitment to me, and I don't take it lightly. Receive my adoration, my good shepherd, for laying down Your life for me.

Confession

Jesus, my good shepherd, I realize that my thoughts and actions must cause You to scratch Your head in bewilderment. Despite being the recipient of Your continual care, I still seek to roam in places of great danger. I confess that I also neglect a heart of gratitude for the many times You have guarded me from dangers which were meant to destroy me, and for the other times You have pulled me from the edge of a cliff that I had gone to on my own. Forgive me for failing to listen to You. Forgive me for choosing not to follow You in all that I do. Forgive me for taking for granted the healing ointments of Your grace and mercy that You use to restore me from the consequences of my wrong choices.

Thanksgiving

Jesus, I thank You that You are my good shepherd. I am grateful that You carry me in Your arms. You are gentle, not rough. You are caring, not distant. As it's written in Isaiah 40:11, "Like a shepherd He will tend His flock, in His arm He will gather the lambs and carry them in His bosom; He will gently lead the nursing ewes." Thank You for gently leading me and carrying me close to Your heart. When I am weary, You stoop down and lift me so that I can go farther in Your loving arms. Thank You for shepherding me and not giving up on me time and time again.

Supplication

Jesus, help me listen to You as my good shepherd. Listening to You and following You will give me the ability to avoid so many pitfalls in this life. I am often stubborn, Jesus. You know that. So I ask that Your gentle qualities as a good shepherd will proactively guide me away from temptations and disaster while simultaneously steering me toward Your purpose and plans.

5

I AM

*Jesus said to them, "Truly, truly, I say to you,
before Abraham was born, I am."*

JOHN 8:58

Adoration

Jesus, the name I Am is the name which caused the Jews to seek Your death. Through it, You revealed that You are God. You are before the foundation of all time. You are the Creator of all things. I adore You because, as God, You did not remove Yourself from the day-in and day-out experiences of Your creation. Rather, You, the great I Am, joined us in it. You boldly proclaimed Your deity to ears and hearts that refused to believe You. Yet their rejection only led to the greatest display of Your deity—the death and resurrection of a sinless God for sinful humanity. I praise You, Jesus—the I Am who was, is, and will forever be.

Confession

Jesus, I confess that this name does not get the attention from me that it should. You are the great I Am. You are Creator. Healer. Ruler. You have gifted me this experience of life. Yet I often go through my days without paying You the attention You deserve. I am sorry. Forgive me for the pride that causes me to somehow think this is okay. You are the powerful I Am who deserves my highest honor and praise, and yet sometimes I barely drag myself to church, or I simply flip open my Bible to mark it off my list. I do not deserve to have the opportunity to speak with someone as high as You are. Yet You patiently wait for me to do so each and every day. Forgive me.

Thanksgiving

Jesus, thank You for revealing Your nature to those we would least expect. As You walked this earth, You kept it hidden from the people who thought themselves to be wise. Yet You let a Samaritan woman in on who You are when You spent some moments with her around a well. We read in John 4:25-26, "The woman said to Him, 'I know that Messiah is coming (He who is called Christ); when that One comes, He will declare all things to us.' Jesus said to her, 'I who speak to you am He.'" You told her, "I am He." No fanfare surrounded Your words. No attention-seeking platform set them up. You spoke with an obscure woman from an enemy tribe, and when she caught on to who You are, You leaned in as if telling her a secret that You had been wanting to shout from the highest mountaintops: "I am." Thank You for the humility and approachability You have which allow me to know the great I Am.

Supplication

Jesus, may I give You the honor that is due You. May I know You as closely as the Samaritan woman or Martha, to whom You also revealed the name I Am, as recorded in John 11:25. I ask that You give me the opportunity to discover what it feels like to have You lean over to me and remind me, "I am." To feel the calm rush over me as

I realize that the one who made it all, knows it all, controls it all, and has made Himself accessible to me at any moment in time. And that He loves me. That's my prayer, Jesus, the great I Am. I want to hear You in such a way that makes You smile.

Lord is it You That is ~~Just~~ waking me   He says
up early to spend time w/ You — I Am "

    Is it me or You that is waking me
    up early — He says I Am.   He says

wash me cleanse me — I'm
commune w/ me — I Am
Help me — I Am
Show me — guide me — I Am
Heal me — I Am
provide for me — I Am
protect me — I Am

6

Holy and Righteous One

You disowned the Holy and Righteous One and
asked for a murderer to be granted to you.

Acts 3:14

Adoration

Jesus, I lift up Your name as the holy and righteous one and give You praise from the deepest part of my heart. Your holiness and righteousness set You apart from all others. You and You alone can claim such in Your original form. Because of Your sacrifice, I am righteous in You—but I cannot claim righteousness in my original form. None of us can. You are the only holy and righteous one from the beginning of time. I worship You and cry out like the angels in Isaiah 6:3, "Holy, Holy, Holy, is the LORD of hosts, the whole earth is full of His glory." Fill me with Your glory as I focus my thoughts on You.

Confession

Jesus, the holy and righteous one, forgive me, for I am a sinner. I am not holy. I am not righteous. Not on my own. The holiness and righteousness I have has been transmitted to me from You. I confess that I am guilty and deserving of eternal separation from You, and yet it is from Your holiness that I derive my own. Forgive me for taking that lightly far too often and failing to live with the right heart toward You, filled with gratitude, awe, humility, and motivation to serve You.

Thanksgiving

Jesus, thank You for offering up Your holiness and righteousness so that I can gain access to God through You. As it says in 2 Corinthians 5:21, "He made Him who knew no sin to be sin on our behalf, so that we might become the righteousness of God in Him." You who knew no sin became sin so that I could be forgiven. Thank You for Your great humility that gave You the strength to do that. Thank You for Your great love that motivated You to provide the way for my salvation. Thank You for the gift of walking in the power, purity, and protection of Your holiness and righteousness as I travel the pathways of my life.

Supplication

Jesus, when the Jews rejected you as the holy and righteous one and asked for the release of the murderer Barabbas instead, it was an obvious rejection. Yet there are multiple ways I can marginalize You in my life that may not be so obvious. I do this when I choose to listen to other people's perspectives rather than Yours, or when I seek other people's approval more than Yours, or when I dishonor You with my choices and words, or when I choose to spend more time on fruitless activities—or even sinful ones—rather than recognizing You as the owner and source of all my time, talents, and treasures. When I refuse to steward my life under Your rule, I also disown You as the holy and righteous one. Jesus, my prayer is that You will guide me away from these decisions and toward a greater understanding of what it means to use the life You've given me in order to bring You glory and others good and to advance Your kingdom on earth.

Ruler

*You, Bethlehem, land of Judah, are by no means least
among the leaders of Judah; for out of you shall come
forth a Ruler who will shepherd My people Israel.*

Matthew 2:6

Adoration

Jesus, You are the great ruler over all, and I trust Your power over
my life. I can rest knowing that You are in charge. You cause all things
to work together for good in my life as I seek You and love You with
all my heart. You maneuver all circumstances to bring about Your
intended purposes according to the direction of Your rule. I can take
a deep breath as I trust in Your hand over all. I can relax in the finality of Your decisions. I praise You for taking so much worry and stress
off me just through my knowing this name of Yours. You are ruler
over all.

Confession

Jesus, there are so many benefits I get to experience because You
are the ultimate ruler. I get to enjoy greater rest as I trust in You. I get
to see You override and overturn things that are unjust or in opposition to me when they go against Your will. But even though I am

the recipient of so much goodness because of Your rule, I sometimes attempt to rule things myself. I do this by trying to make my own decisions apart from Your will. In that way, I am declaring myself as owner rather than as manager or steward over what You've given me. I'm sorry, and I confess this to You now as I seek Your forgiveness and extended grace.

Thanksgiving

Jesus, thank You for seeing to every minute detail of my life through the expression of Your rule. Thank You for guiding me according to Your perfect path. Thank You for the patience You show me time and time again when I deviate from Your rule and You gently guide me back. Thank You that You are not some distant God who leaves me on my own. Rather, You are intimately close and hold everything together. Thank You for caring so deeply for me that You give me the blessing of Your rule.

Supplication

Jesus, I ask that You help me identify areas in my life where I am not yielding to Your rule as I should. You are the ruler over all, and yet I am acting in rebellion when I choose to go my own way. I want to abide in You, and that means aligning myself under You according to Your overarching rule. Help me have the self-restraint, personal discipline, and power to do just that. I humble myself beneath Your rule, Jesus, and ask that You will bring forth the full blessing of the expression of Your rule in my life.

ALPHA AND OMEGA

"I am the Alpha and the Omega," says the Lord God,
"who is and who was and who is to come, the Almighty."

REVELATION 1:8

Adoration

Jesus, You are the Alpha and the Omega—the first and the last. In You all things have their beginning and all things have their end. Even me. I am Yours. Jesus, I adore You and honor You for how vast You are. You are above all, over all, before all, and after all. You are the sum total, as well as the details in between. I honor Your greatness and expansiveness in how You are able to marry time with Your intentions as You give us a place within which to live and carry out Your plans for our lives. You are beyond my understanding, and I give You praise.

Confession

Jesus, I confess that while I often look to You for comfort or peace, I don't always look to You as the initiator of everything in my life. I choose to move forward in my own strength based on my own ideas rather than trust Your leading. But Your name as the Alpha and Omega means You are to be the initiator and completer of all things in my life. As Colossians 1:18 says, "He is also head of the body, the church; and He is the beginning, the firstborn from the dead, so that He Himself will come to have first place in everything." When I fail to honor Your name in this way, I remove You from the first place You are to have in my life. Please forgive me.

Thanksgiving

Jesus, thank You that You don't forget how I feel in Your presence. Thank You for using Your power and position as an avenue for comfort. Thank You that I no longer have to fear when I trust in Your name of Alpha and Omega, as You reveal in Revelation 1:17, which says, "When I saw Him, I fell at His feet like a dead man. And He placed His right hand on me, saying, 'Do not be afraid; I am the first and the last.'" Thank You for the grace You show in the midst of Your might, allowing me to trust in Your control and preeminence over all.

Supplication

Jesus, You have called all things into being. You are the Creator, and I am Your follower. Isaiah 41:4 says of You, "Who has performed and accomplished it, calling forth the generations from the beginning? 'I, the LORD, am the first, and with the last. I am He.'" I cannot steal Your credit nor Your glory. Everything You have brought about in my life is because of Your name, Alpha and Omega. You bookend my accomplishments with Your power. I ask that You give me a right heart to acknowledge You more aptly according to the credit due You, so I won't seek to hijack Your glory through a displacement of honor onto myself.

ADVOCATE

My little children, I am writing these things to you so that you may not sin. And if anyone sins, we have an Advocate with the Father, Jesus Christ the righteous.

1 JOHN 2:1

Adoration

Jesus, You are my advocate. You have been positioned to provide the way for me to receive the forgiveness of my sins, which I need so desperately. First Timothy 2:5 tells me that this name belongs only to You: "There is one God, and one mediator also between God and men, the man Christ Jesus." I adore You and worship You for Your humility and strength which allow You to live out the full expression of this name. I honor Your grace, patience, and compassion which led You to take my place, fulfilling all of sin's punishments for me.

Confession

Jesus, the blood of Abel reveals the true propensity of the heart of mankind. It is a heart that is deceitful above all else. I confess that I crave attention, notoriety, and position, a craving which led Cain to brutally slay his brother, Abel. Jealousy moves through my veins, tainting my blood with the sin of self-importance. Yet You are my advocate. You stand before the Father, offering a pure and acceptable sacrifice. As Hebrews 12:24 says, "To Jesus, the mediator of a new covenant, and to the sprinkled blood, which speaks better than the blood of Abel." I confess I need this forgiveness over all of me.

Thanksgiving

Thank You, Jesus, for being my advocate. Thank You for offering on my behalf the sacrifices and gifts which please the Father. Your life is my life because You are the source of my life, both for now and in eternity. Hebrews 8:1-3 speaks of the power of Your name when it says, "We have such a high priest, who has taken His seat at the right hand of the throne of the Majesty in the heavens, a minister in the sanctuary and in the true tabernacle, which the Lord pitched, not man. For every high priest is appointed to offer both gifts and sacrifices; so it is necessary that this high priest also have something to offer." I thank You, Jesus, my advocate, for loving me from Your throne on high.

Supplication

Jesus, You have modeled what it means to be an advocate. You have daily gone before the throne of God on my behalf, defending me and delivering me. The care You have shown me is the reason I am here today. I want to follow You as Your kingdom disciple in such a way that I bring to others a portion of the love You bring to me. Make me an advocate for those who are in need. Proverbs 31:8-9 calls me to "open [my] mouth for the mute, for the rights of all the unfortunate. Open [my] mouth, judge righteously, and defend the rights of the afflicted and needy." Open my eyes to see where and how I can live out the full meaning of this verse in order to model Your love to those in need.

CHIEF SHEPHERD

When the Chief Shepherd appears,
you will receive the unfading crown of glory.

1 PETER 5:4

Adoration

Jesus, not only are You the good shepherd, but You are also the chief shepherd. You are in charge. You are over all. You hold all things together according to Your perfect plan and kingdom agenda. I worship You for Your power, might, superintendence, and greatness. I honor You for Your name above all names, that of the chief shepherd.

Confession

Jesus, I am guilty of being very much like a sheep. I do stray. I tend to think my way is better than Your way. I forget to follow You, my chief shepherd. I confess to You that this name is not a name I call on often, unless I am in a pinch and need to be delivered from the edge of a cliff, or I have wandered too deep into the darkness of a valley. But Your role as chief shepherd is that of guiding me so I don't even get to the edge of a cliff or feel alone in the valley. You are with me. I am sorry for not recognizing this as often as I should.

Thanksgiving

Jesus, thank You for taking full ownership and responsibility for my life. Even though I am apt to forget that reality, it holds true nonetheless. Thank You for being my chief shepherd. You have a perfect path planned for me if I will just follow You there. Thank You for reminding me of this truth today. Thank You that Psalm 23 is Your love letter to me, reminding me in verse 1 that "the LORD is my shepherd, I shall not want."

Supplication

Jesus, I ask that You lead me beside still waters, as it says in Psalm 23:2. As my chief shepherd, will You make it very clear to me where You are leading me and show me the places I can go in my life which will bring rest and comfort and peace? When issues arise, remind me that I have nothing to fear—because "perfect love casts out fear," as it says in 1 John 4:18, and Your love is perfect toward me. I ask that You make me more aware of the goodness and loving-kindness You have stationed around me so that I can access the blessings found in embracing both.

CREATOR

All things came into being through Him, and apart from Him nothing came into being that has come into being.

JOHN 1:3

Adoration

Jesus, I adore You as Creator. This name gives me insight into Your power, position, and authority. As John 1:1-3 says when speaking of You, "In the beginning was the Word, and the Word was with God, and the Word was God. He was in the beginning with God. All things came into being through Him, and apart from Him nothing came into being that has come into being." Nothing has come about that didn't first pass through Your fingers as the Creator. Everything owes its existence to You, including me. You are a wonder and power, Jesus the Creator.

Confession

Jesus, how silly I must look to You when I seek to create my own reality or dream up my own dreams. I confess that not only do I neglect to tap into Your power, but I also often try to usurp it by attempting to invent my own destiny. What's worse, when You do create things through me, I more often than not bask in the credit. Forgive me for dishonoring this name, Jesus the Creator.

Thanksgiving

Jesus, Scripture tells us in Colossians 1:16, "By Him all things were created, both in the heavens and on earth, visible and invisible, whether thrones or dominions or rulers or authorities—all things have been created through Him and for Him." Not only have You created all things visible and invisible, but You have created them for You. All thrones, dominions, rulers, and authorities are sourced in You as the Creator. Thank You for Your creation and for Your creative powers as expressed both in and through my life.

Supplication

Jesus, create in me and through me exactly what You want for my life. For starters, "create in me a clean heart, O God, and renew a steadfast spirit within me," as Psalm 51:10 says. After that, Jesus, create in me a vision that is in accordance with Your plan for my life. Create ideas in my mind that will give me the direction to follow. Create a passion in my spirit for pursuing You as well as loving others as You do. Create the relationships I need that will give me the opportunity to influence others for good. I ask for all of this according to Your name as the Creator.

12

Dayspring

*Through the tender mercy of our God, with which
the Dayspring from on high has visited us.*

LUKE 1:78 NKJV

Adoration

Jesus, You are the dayspring from on high who has come and visited us. You are the bright and morning sun who shines light on us all. Your light ushers in a new day, and Your presence ushers in a new season. Winter can feel as if it drags on too long for many of us living our days on earth, but You are the promise of an ongoing spring. I praise You for the joy You bring through Your presence. I honor You for the delight of who You are. You have the power to transform a dark, cold, and dreary life in just one moment with the radiance of Your being.

Confession

Jesus, I know that I complain of the challenges I face in life. I complain and am embittered by them far too frequently. Like experiencing a cold spell that has gone on too long, I forget to look toward the spring and sunshine about to hit the horizon and focus instead on the clouds of the moment I am in. Forgive me for failing to call on You as the dayspring of my heart. You can melt away my misery when I spend just one moment in Your presence. Forgive me for neglecting to look to You and focusing on my circumstances instead.

Thanksgiving

Jesus, thank You for the refreshing love You bring to me through this name—the dayspring from on high. Thank You for the warmth of Your presence that I can feel on my face when I bask in the unchanging flow of Your love, grace, and tender mercies. As a potted flower placed in a home bends toward the window in order to stretch and feel the sun, may I bend toward You in all I do, knowing that I receive the nourishment for life itself in the calming strength of Your provision.

Supplication

Jesus, will You transform the difficulties I am facing with Your light? Will You bring warmth into my cold heart? Break through the clouds of doubt which linger over me—the fog caused by worry and the freezing rain of anxiety. Break through it all with the brightness of Your name, and may I feel the instant joy that comes from Your warmth surrounding me. I choose to bask in Your glory, Your radiance, and Your peace. I choose to receive my strength from You as my source. Remind me of this in those times when I forget to look to You for Your light, Jesus. Somehow capture my attention or gaze so that I can shift my focus onto You. When I do, I will be enriched with Your provision and fed with Your peace.

13

Branch of the Lord

In that day the Branch of the Lord will be beautiful and glorious, and the fruit of the earth will be the pride and the adornment of the survivors of Israel.

Isaiah 4:2

Adoration

Jesus, You are the branch of the Lord. You are beautiful and glorious, the pride and the adornment of my life. Not only did You create the earth, but You are also the fruit of the earth. I worship You for Your ability to produce fruit in the lives of Your followers. Though we often stray from You and fail to abide in You, You faithfully draw us back to You according to Your tender mercies and loving care. May You receive the credit that is due You. May I recognize You as the source of all that is produced and not forget to give You the honor for every good thing and perfect gift You provide me. My prayer is that You fully feel my love for You and my gratitude to You.

Confession

Jesus, You are the branch of the Lord, but You have also called and created me to be a branch after Your likeness. I am to model the fruitfulness You have demonstrated. I confess that I often pull away from

You and then become a fruitless branch. As John 15:6 says, "If anyone does not abide in Me, he is thrown away as a branch and dries up; and they gather them, and cast them into the fire and they are burned." Forgive me for failing to abide in You. Forgive me for failing to honor You as the branch of the Lord, holy and righteous. I ask for Your grace and mercy to such a degree that will allow me to experience the fruitfulness You Yourself produce as the branch of the Lord.

Thanksgiving

Jesus, You tell us in John 15:5, "I am the vine, you are the branches; he who abides in Me and I in him, he bears much fruit, for apart from Me you can do nothing." As the branch of the Lord, You know firsthand the importance of abiding. As You and the Father are one, You have called me to be one in You. Thank You for giving me the opportunity to tap into You as my source. Thank You for freely providing me all I need to bear fruit. Thank You for making fruit bearing simple enough for me to do regularly merely through abiding in You. You have set the example of what a branch of the Lord is to do. It is to bear rich and lasting spiritual fruit. Thank You for giving me such a high calling in You so that I may know this name of Yours more closely.

Supplication

Jesus, You have called me to live a holy life as You are holy. I seek this life in You. As You reflect the Father in all that You are, I want to reflect You. Romans 11:16 says, "If the first piece of dough is holy, the lump is also; and if the root is holy, the branches are too." You are not only the branch of the Lord, but You are also the root for all other branches to tap into. When I am abiding in You fully and completely, my thoughts are set upon pleasing You, knowing You, and reflecting Your glory to others. I ask that You give me the grace and honor of living a life that makes You smile because of the holy fruit You are able to produce through me.

14

FORERUNNER

Jesus has entered as a forerunner for us, having become a
high priest forever according to the order of Melchizedek.

HEBREWS 6:20

Adoration

Jesus, You went before us to prepare the way. Your sacrifice provided me with salvation. You are the high priest according to the order of Melchizedek. I honor You as the forerunner. I worship You for Your ability to make a way out of no way. There was at one point no method for me to reach the throne of God. Yet You provided that way as the forerunner. As John the Baptist went ahead of You to call people to repentance, You have gone ahead of us all to provide the satisfaction for that repentance. I praise and thank You for this gift.

Confession

Jesus, I often forget what had to happen in order for You to provide a way for me to be saved. I often neglect to acknowledge how difficult it had to have been for You to be the forerunner. A forerunner is one who goes it alone. It is an isolating name to live out. You had no one to give You encouragement as You suffered for the sins of humanity on the cross. Yet, somehow, I forget this reality and live as if I am entitled to what You have provided for me. Forgive me for my arrogance, Jesus. Forgive me for my lack of compassion toward You and my lack of gratitude for something that had to have been excruciatingly difficult to offer. You were forsaken on the cross. Alone. Forgive me for marginalizing Your pain when I treat the cross and Your sacrifice casually in my heart—and especially when I sin in spite of all it cost You.

Thanksgiving

Jesus, thank You for Your willingness to serve all of us as the forerunner. Thank You for bearing the loneliness, isolation, and difficulties that arise from going it alone. Thank You for the great compassion You have toward me in that You comfort me when I feel alone. No one knows what it truly means to be alone and rejected as well as You do. And yet, rather than make me feel guilty when I complain or am sad due to my own circumstances, You make Yourself available to comfort me. Thank You for Your selfless love as shown when You lived out the role of forerunner so that I would never have to go it alone.

Supplication

Jesus, help me honor You and Your name more fully in all that I do. Let my thoughts, words, and actions reflect a spirit overwhelmed with gratitude for You. I ask that You give me wisdom on how to best steward the time, talents, and treasures You have placed under my care in such a way that dignifies the difficulties You suffered as the forerunner in order to allow me this opportunity to serve. I hope that You will be pleased with my commitment to You and that, somehow, it will bring You joy. I humbly bow before You to thank You for all You have done for me.

15

Bread Out of Heaven

Jesus then said to them,
"Truly, truly, I say to you,
it is not Moses who has given you the bread
out of heaven, but it is My Father who gives
you the true bread out of heaven."

John 6:32

Adoration

Jesus, in You are the nutrients for all life. You are the true bread out of heaven. You provide all I need for me to live out the purpose I have in You. I praise You for Your completeness. I honor You for Your provision. I look to You to feed me and fill me with both comfort and strength. Not only are You the true bread out of heaven who supplies me with all I need, but You also supply all of creation with what it needs. I worship You for the way You hold the earth together and have established the seasons according to Your purposes. You water the fields so they bear fruit. You nourish the animals so they reproduce after their own kind. You provide the sunlight which gives life. You are the true bread out of heaven by which all of creation finds its source of life.

Confession

Jesus, I confess that I often seek to fill up on junk food rather than You, the true bread out of heaven. I feed myself with the vain philosophies of this world and entertain myself with fruitless gossip. Jesus, I look to people for wisdom when I should be looking to You. Yet, despite my turning to that which does not sustain me time and time again, You are always available to me as the true bread out of heaven. You patiently wait for me to realize my lack of nourishment and my need for real food. Forgive me for dismissing You as my source far too frequently.

Thanksgiving

Jesus, thank You for filling me to the point that I am full. Thank You that whenever I need You, You are there. You are consistent, reliable, present, and comprised of all I need in order to grow according to the power that works in me, which is You. Thank You that You know what is best for me and seek to give me that rather than the things which will merely satisfy me for a moment. Thank You for putting up with me in those times when I stuff myself on the world's wisdom and goods. You never turn Your back to me. Rather, You invite me to eat of You, the true bread out of heaven.

Supplication

Jesus, I need to spend more time in Your Word, feeding on You, the true bread out of heaven. Help me cultivate a regular time in Scripture. Remind me when I have gone too long without meditating on Your Word. Jesus, feed me with the nourishment that I need. Convict me when I am wasting my time on that which is junk food and of little value to me. Help me create greater margin in my days and in my mind so that I find myself returning to You and Your Word more frequently. I would never think of eating once every few weeks and then never eating again. Help me never to think of abiding in

You, the true bread out of heaven, only for a short time and then not again for many days, weeks, or months. Rescue me from the tyranny of being too busy so that I make filling up on the true bread out of heaven a more consistent part of my day.

Amen

*To the angel of the church in Laodicea write: The Amen,
the faithful and true Witness, the Beginning of the creation
of God, says this: "I know your deeds."*

Adoration

Jesus, You are the great Amen. In You I find the true meaning
of faithfulness, reliability, authority, power, and truth. It is recorded
that, as You walked on the earth, You often began what You had to
say with the power of this name. About 70 times You said, "*Amen lego
humin*," which translates to mean, "Truly, I say to you." Not only are
You the Amen, but You express the authority of this truth and reality in all You do. You are true. You are holy. You are faithful. You are
present. You are consistent. You are full of grace, power, and strength.
You are the full manifestation of the name Amen.

Confession

Jesus, please forgive me when I use this name without the reverence due You. The word *amen* has become almost like a ritualistic tag
to place at the end of prayers. But this is Your name, and it reflects
the qualities which make You stand apart from all else. I confess that

I often neglect to honor this name of Yours, or I question it when I doubt Your faithfulness. Forgive me for doubting You when things go wrong in my life. Forgive me for questioning Your power when situations don't go how I had hoped. Forgive me for failing to trust in the one who is the Amen, the faithful and true witness.

Thanksgiving

Thank You, Jesus, for caring enough to remain faithful. Thank You that You are reliable. If You took even a moment away from Your role as the Amen, the earth itself would fail to be held together. It is You who holds all things together. It is Your name that testifies to Your importance and significance. Thank You for remaining faithful even when I am faithless. You have shown me what consistency looks like, what truth looks like. Help me show You my gratitude by modeling my life after You.

Supplication

Jesus, give me the grace to know this name of Yours, Amen, more intimately. I want to know this name like the name of a close friend. Every time I say, "Amen," let me be mindful of Your faithfulness, commitment, and truth. Open my eyes to areas in my life where I am failing to reflect this name of Yours as an image bearer of who You are. Convict me when truth, faithfulness, and reliability do not define what I do or say. Draw me into a loving relationship with You at such a depth that I can confidently rest in You and in such a way that gives me the grace to be faithful and truthful myself. I want to be like You as the Amen—a faithful and true witness of God's holiness, power, perfection, and rule.

17

AUTHOR AND PERFECTER OF FAITH

Fixing our eyes on Jesus,
the author and perfecter
of faith, who for the joy set before Him
endured the cross, despising the shame,
and has sat down at the right
hand of the throne of God.

HEBREWS 12:2

Adoration

Jesus, I adore You as the author and perfecter of faith. For the joy set before You, You endured the cross. You despised the shame, but You pressed through, knowing that glory was on the other side of pain. You have "sat down at the right hand of the throne of God," where You perfect the faith of all who place their trust in You. I worship You for Your strength to press through while despising the shame You bore. I praise You for the restraint You displayed when You could have taken Yourself off the cross, choosing to endure instead. I honor Your commitment to the purpose of perfecting the faith of sinful humanity, a role only You could carry out.

Confession

Jesus, I confess that I often want to be the author of my life. I demonstrate this by making my own decisions without consulting You and Your perspective prior to moving forward. Then, when things go wrong, I get frustrated. Yet, if I would follow You from the start and obey what You have written for me to live out, I would not waste so much time on the wrong path. Forgive me when I forget this name of Yours which designates You as the author and perfecter of faith. Forgive me for seeking my own way outside of Your will and kingdom agenda.

Thanksgiving

Jesus, thank You for perfecting my imperfections. Thank You for providing me with the way for living a righteous life as I hide myself in You. Thank You that I do not need to live with constant guilt and shame because You took away my guilt and bore my shame. Your perfection is what makes me whole, and I thank You that I can rest knowing I am complete in You. Thank You, also, for designing my life intentionally. As an author sets out to write a book with themes, progression, and development, You have authored my faith according to the best possible plan to bring You the greatest glory and deliver the greatest good to others. In this, I find satisfaction and peace.

Supplication

Jesus, help me let go of my failures and imperfections as I release them into Your loving grace. Help me live in the peace that comes from identifying myself in Your perfection of my faith. Give me confidence as I approach God's throne to boldly ask for anything in Your name that falls within Your will. May my heart find joy in knowing that I do not have to strive after a perfection I can never achieve because Your name declares that You have already accomplished this for me. You are the author and perfecter of my faith, and I love You entirely because of this great gift.

Great High Priest

Since we have a great high priest
who has passed through the heavens,
Jesus the Son of God,
let us hold fast our confession.

Hebrews 4:14

Adoration

Jesus, I adore You not only because You bring me refreshment and blessing in Your role as the Great High Priest, but also because You bring me a unique level of intimacy with the Father and a stability for my soul. I see this in Hebrews 6:19-20, which says, "This hope we have as an anchor of the soul, a hope both sure and steadfast and one which enters within the veil, where Jesus has entered as a forerunner for us, having become a high priest forever according to the order of Melchizedek." Jesus, You are the anchor for my soul. An anchor holds a boat steady. When the boat drops anchor, the anchor then keeps the boat in place despite how windy or stormy it might be. Even though the boat may be rocking, it never leaves its location because the anchor holds. Jesus, You are the anchor that holds my life steady, and I worship You for it.

Confession

Jesus, please forgive me for worrying, stressing, or feeling anxious. You have commanded me not to do these things. Not only that, but Your role as the Great High Priest has given me all I need to rest and not fret. When I worry, I am neglecting this name of Yours. Show me grace and mercy for those times that I forget to apply the meaning of this name to my everyday life.

Thanksgiving

Jesus, an interesting thing about when the priest during the Old Testament times would enter into Your presence—it is said that they would have to tie a rope around his ankle in case he did something wrong. If he was struck dead, no one could go in and get him because no one else was authorized to enter into the holiest place. So if the priest died, they had to literally pull him out with a rope. But Jesus, You have paid the price for my access. I thank You that Your righteousness has been imputed to me. I no longer need the rope because Your name has made the pathway to the Father open to me. First John 2:2 tells me, "He Himself is the propitiation for our sins; and not for ours only, but also for those of the whole world." Thank You for the access You give me.

Supplication

Jesus, because Your name is Great High Priest, I can hold tight to my faith. I can hold fast to my confession and not give up. I can do this because I know I have somebody positioned for me who understands my struggles and pain and has made a way for me to approach the one who can address them. There is no category of life that You have not also experienced, my Great High Priest. You know what it is to be lonely. You know what it is to be rejected. You know what it is to be abandoned, physically beat up, hurt. You know how it feels to cry, to weep, to shed tears of blood because the pain is so deep. You know what it is to be betrayed. You know what it is to be thirsty, hungry, tempted, attacked, spurned, and looked down upon. You can sympathize. You understand. And I can access that sympathy and compassion by drawing near to You, my Great High Priest.

19

LIFE

Jesus said to him, "I am the way, and the truth, and the life; no one comes to the Father but through Me."

JOHN 14:6

Adoration

Jesus, You are the way, the truth, and the life. In You is the source of life itself. Without You, nothing would be able to survive. Not even for a moment in time. You hold all things together through Your great power as You sit outside of the creation You made but also abide within it. This name ascribes to You all praise, honor, and glory because there is nothing more critical to each of us than life. Whether that be life here on earth or eternal life, we only exist because You give it. I worship You as the source of my life both for now—in every moment of every day—and also for eternity, as I place my faith in You for the salvation of my soul.

Confession

Jesus, I confess that I take life for granted far too many times. I take my life here on earth for granted, but I also take my eternal life for granted. I do this through actions which dismiss You. These might not be outright dismissals, but rather more subtle ones where I simply go throughout my day without acknowledging You. You are the source of all I am, standing by patiently, lovingly while I navigate through life with my thoughts on everything but You. Please forgive my immature chasing of distractions. Forgive me for forgetting that You are my life, and in You is found the abundant life which I desire.

Thanksgiving

Jesus, thank You for my life. Thank You for the air I breathe. Thank You that You keep my body functioning without me even having to think about it or tell my body what to do. You have given me a body that does so many miraculous things moment by moment. I am not even aware of all that my body does to sustain the life You've given me. Thank You for Your wisdom. Thank You for Your divine design. Thank You for trusting me with the high calling of stewarding this life I've been given to live out in Your name and for Your glory.

Supplication

Jesus, when a loved one passes away or when I hear of some tragedy, my focus on life itself is heightened in my heart and mind. It is in these times that I thank You for the gift You have given me. Then, as life goes on, I sometimes move away from that awareness and fall back into a spirit of complaint or even boredom as I go through my days, rather than appreciating each moment You've placed in my care. I ask that You help me treasure this name of Yours, Jesus. Help me treasure it not only when it is brought to the forefront of my mind through tragedy or trials, but also in the everydayness of life. May I honor You by honoring Your name, which is life itself. Life is a gift. Help me treat it as such.

20

LAMB OF GOD

The next day he saw Jesus coming to him and said,
"Behold, the Lamb of God who takes away the sin of the
world!"

JOHN 1:29

Adoration

I adore You, Jesus, as "the Lamb of God who takes away the sin of the world." I honor You for Your sacrifice, a sacrifice that is pure enough to be counted as righteousness. There is now no condemnation for me because of Your blood sacrifice on my behalf. Not only did You allow me to be forgiven, but You removed my guilt. I worship You for Your grace and mercy, which enable me to ascend in my identity to where You are seated at the right hand of God in the heavenlies. My identity is now in You because of this great name of Yours, the Lamb of God.

Confession

Jesus, You are the Lamb of God who takes away my sin. I understand that God the Father is holy. He is just. He is not merely reactional when it comes to His response to sin. He doesn't just lose it and get mad. Rather, His wrath is tied to His justice, and His justice is part of His nature. And while He doesn't prefer wrath, He can't skip justice. He has to exercise it. Thus, out of His great mercy and grace, He came up with a way to avert His wrath. The blood of the Lamb—Your sacrifice, Jesus—averts judgment based on the Father's justice. I confess my sins before You as I receive the free forgiveness You offer.

Thanksgiving

Thank You for the life I have which is rooted in You—the Lamb of God, the sin bearer and remover of my shame. Thank You, Jesus, for the kindness You have shown me despite my sins. Thank You that I do not need to fear where I will spend eternity because I am assured of salvation through the sacrificial Lamb. Thank You that I do not need to fear rejection or the wrath of a holy God because Your righteousness has been imputed to me. When the Father looks at me, He sees the blood of the Lamb. He sees Your perfection overriding my sinfulness. Thank You for Your provision of hope and peace through Your shed blood.

Supplication

Jesus, may I never belittle You by failing to give You the honor You have earned in my heart by Your sacrifice as the Lamb of God. May I never be so ashamed of it that I refuse to tell others the way that they, too, can receive eternal life. Show me how to better honor what You have done as the Lamb of God so that my life will be used by You to bring You glory. I seek a greater commitment in myself toward uplifting Your name. Show me how to live that out as I steward my time, talents, and treasures under You.

21

IMMANUEL

The Lord Himself will give you a sign:
Behold, a virgin will be with child and bear a son,
and she will call His name Immanuel.

ISAIAH 7:14

Adoration

Jesus, although You are beyond all things, above all things, over all things, and in control of all things, You humbled Yourself to be born of a virgin so that God could be with us. The name Immanuel is a name I hold dear to my heart because it is the name which says You came near. I worship You for Your willingness to come near. I worship You for Your power to come near. I worship You for Your ability to come near. May You rejoice and be glad in my worship, and may it remind You of the shepherds who also worshiped You on the very night when divinity entered earth in the form of a man, Immanuel.

Confession

Jesus, You are near, and You have made it possible for me to be near You. When I am near You, I experience peace, rest, hope, calm, and clarity. When I am distant, those things fade away like dusk into the night. Jesus, I confess that I do not always abide near enough to

You to access all You have for me. Forgive me for feeling that I don't need to make You a priority and for those times when that is what I indicate to You by my thoughts and actions. Have mercy on me for failing to take full advantage of Your nearness, Immanuel.

Thanksgiving

Jesus, thank You that even though You created kings, dominions, rulers, and authorities, You have also created a way to spend time with someone like me. Thank You that the name Immanuel reminds me of Your willingness and desire to know me. I want to experience the fullness of You through this name. Thank You for giving me that opportunity.

Supplication

Jesus, help me know the heart of God the Father in a way and at a depth I have never known before. Help me feel the presence of the Holy Spirit in a closeness that will cause me to marvel. Help me fully embrace the meaning of this name, Immanuel, so that Your nearness is not wasted on apathy or, even worse, rejection. I seek Your closeness. May I be considered a friend of God because of the path You have opened through this name, Immanuel. May I be one of those who gets to know the secrets of God because we are so close. Help me prioritize my time in such a way that gives me the greatest possible margin for knowing the full manifestation of the name Immanuel.

22

KING

Rejoice greatly, O daughter of Zion!
Shout in triumph, O daughter of Jerusalem!
Behold, your king is coming to you;
He is just and endowed with salvation,
humble, and mounted on a donkey,
even on a colt, the foal of a donkey.

ZECHARIAH 9:9

Adoration

Jesus, I shouldn't be surprised that when You were ready to reveal Your kingship, You told Your disciples to get You a donkey, since it had been prophesied that the divine King would ride on one. I shouldn't be shocked that the magi came to worship You after Your birth, claiming that You were born King of the Jews. When John the Baptist announced Your arrival, as recorded in Matthew 3:2, he phrased it in terms the nation of Israel could understand: "Repent, for the kingdom of heaven is at hand." And when You began preaching, You stepped onto the stage of history and said the same thing, as Matthew 4:17 attests: "From that time Jesus began to preach and say, 'Repent, for the kingdom of heaven is at hand.'"

Furthermore, as You sent Your disciples to preach, You told them to proclaim the kingdom of God had arrived. The King has come. I adore You, King Jesus.

Confession

Jesus, a king rules. It's what a king does. He sets the standard by which all his subjects must adjust. I confess that I don't always look to You as having the authority of a king. Sometimes I take Your Word and see it more as a suggestion than as a command. Forgive me for desiring Your intervention in my life as King but still refusing to follow Your lead in my life. I seek to obey You more. Give me a heart to do that.

Thanksgiving

Thank You, Jesus, that You did not hide this name or Your purpose from us, but rather made them clear in so many ways. In John 18:37, we see You doing just that: "Pilate said to Him, 'So You are a king?' Jesus answered, 'You say correctly that I am a king. For this I have been born, and for this I have come into the world, to testify to the truth. Everyone who is of the truth hears My voice.'" Thank You for giving us the ability to know You as King—because it is in knowing You as King that we can honor and obey You as King.

Supplication

Jesus, I want to see Your kingdom agenda advanced near and far across the entire earth. I want to see You receive the glory and honor that is due You as King. Help me be an integral part of the movement of raising up kingdom followers who love You and proclaim Your kingdom to anyone and everyone who will listen. Give me wisdom on how to best steward my time, talents, and treasures in such a way that causes the greatest expansion of Your kingdom rule over every area of our lives on earth. Let love reign preeminent among us, and let us embrace the unity You have called us to embrace as subjects in Your kingdom.

23

Image of God

The god of this world has blinded the minds
of the unbelieving so that they might
not see the light of the gospel
of the glory of Christ,
who is the image of God.

2 Corinthians 4:4

Adoration

Jesus, You are worthy of all praise, glory, and honor, as You are the image of God. Colossians 1:15 says, "He is the image of the invisible God, the firstborn of all creation." You have made visible to us what we were not able to see. As Exodus 33:18-23 tells us, Moses was only allowed to see the passing of God's back, because to view God's face would undo anyone living in human form. So You willingly came to earth to give us a glimpse of God which we could see and behold. I praise You for Your courage, determination, strength, and love that would motivate You to take on flesh in order to help us identify and come to believe in God. Open the minds that have been blinded by the god of this world, Satan himself, so that they may see the light of the gospel of the glory of Christ, the image of God.

Confession

Jesus, John 1:18 tells us, "No one has seen God at any time; the only begotten God who is in the bosom of the Father, He has explained Him." You have explained God to us in a way that we can comprehend. I am sure there is so much more about God that You could not explain to our finite minds. I am sorry for when I try to put God the Father into a box or into a predetermined concept of who I think He is or should be. I am sorry for neglecting to follow His greatest commands, which are to love Him with my whole heart and to love others as myself. You revealed the manifestation of the keeping of those commands through Your life on earth as the image of God. Forgive me for those times when I stray from the model You set as a standard for me.

Thanksgiving

Thank You, Jesus, for allowing me to live in a dispensation of Your revelation. Thank You that I can come to know God more fully because You have revealed Him to me. Hebrews 1:3 says about You, "He is the radiance of His glory and the exact representation of His nature, and upholds all things by the word of His power." You are the radiance of God's glory, shining the light of love, confidence, peace, and calm. Thank You, Jesus, that I do not need to fear or be anxious because in You dwells all the fullness of deity, and You have chosen to dwell in me.

Supplication

Jesus, in John 10:30 You said of Yourself, "I and the Father are one." Then later in the book of John, You prayed that Your followers would be one as You are one with the Father. I want to pray the same prayer as You. You said in John 17:20-23, "I do not ask on behalf of these alone, but for those also who believe in Me through their word; that they may all be one; even as You, Father, are in Me and I in You, that they also may be in Us, so that the world may believe that You sent Me. The glory which You have given Me I have given to them, that they may be one, just as We are one; I in them and You in Me, that they may be perfected in unity, so that the world may know that You sent Me, and loved them, even as You have loved Me." May I be one in You, and may others be one in You, so that we all may be perfected in unity.

24

LIGHT OF THE WORLD

Jesus again spoke to them, saying,
"I am the Light of the world;
he who follows Me will not
walk in the darkness,
but will have the Light of life."

JOHN 8:12

Adoration

Jesus, You are the light of the world. You walked among us to bring us the light that would cast out the darkness. Those who believe in You become children of the light and know the way in which they are to walk. Those who remain in darkness, deceived by the enemy of this age, do not know in which way they are to walk, and they wind up heading in the wrong direction. You said in John 9:5, "While I am in the world, I am the Light of the world." But You also left Your light so we could access it as a guide and illumination for our own lives, as we read in 1 John 2:8: "The darkness is passing away and the true Light is already shining." You are already shining, even though we get a mere glimpse at the entirety of Your light, for we cannot handle the full, glorious expression in our finite forms.

Confession

Jesus, to reject Your light is to reject wisdom, love, kindness, hope, and eternal life. But that is what so many have done. As John 3:19 says, "This is the judgment, that the Light has come into the world, and men loved the darkness rather than the Light, for their deeds were evil." So many people have chosen darkness over light. Jesus, let me not be one of them. Forgive me for the times I have chosen darkness. Forgive me for those times I have let my mind wander to that which is detrimental to my walk with You. Let Your light shine so brightly in me that it affects all I do and think.

Thanksgiving

Thank You, Jesus, for being the light of the world. Thank You for radiating the full glory of God. Thank You that You enlighten us with Your hope. John 1:9 tells us of You, "There was the true Light which, coming into the world, enlightens every man." You are the true light, and in You is the truth that sets us free. Thank You for giving me the opportunity to choose light over darkness, rather than leaving me to my own demise. I honor You and praise You for the beauty, purity, and blessing of Your light. Receive my thanksgiving and let it bring You great joy.

Supplication

Jesus, I ask that every moment of every day—when I am awake and able to direct my mind—that I will turn my thoughts away from the darkness and onto You. As John 12:36 says, "While you have the Light, believe in the Light, so that you may become sons of Light." I seek to believe in You in such a way that gives me the ability to reflect You and Your love all around me. I want to cherish Your light in such a way that other people see it and begin to desire Your light in their life on a greater scale. I pray that You will give me a platform which allows

me to draw people to Your light and fulfill the purpose You have for
my life. Start with me, Jesus. Start by keeping me—my thoughts,
hopes, dreams, ambitions—in the presence of Your life-giving light.

25

Lord of Lords

*Keep the commandment without stain or reproach
until the appearing of our Lord Jesus Christ, which
He will bring about at the proper time—
He who is the blessed and only Sovereign,
the King of kings and Lord of lords.*

1 Timothy 6:14-15

Adoration

Jesus, You are the Lord of lords. You sit high and lifted up, exalted above all rule and authority. It is Your word that is the final word in all matters. You choose what happens. Your providential hand rules entirely. As Revelation 19:16 states, this name of Yours is sealed on You for all to see: "On His robe and on His thigh He has a name written, "KING OF KINGS, AND LORD OF LORDS." I worship You who reigns on high. I adore You for all You have brought about in creation and continue to hold together in the palm of Your hand. I give You my humble worship as a way of saying "thank you" for allowing me the opportunity to know and love You like I do.

Confession

Jesus, have mercy on me for discrediting You and Your rule over all when I seek to take credit for what You have brought about. The name Lord of lords declares Your position. Forgive me for seeking to usurp Your position in my own thoughts when I focus on myself and start believing that I am the cause of doing good works in my life. It is You who both wills and works in and through me for Your good pleasure, as Philippians 2:13 reminds me. Forgive my audacity in forgetting that truth and patting myself on the back instead.

Thanksgiving

Thank You, Jesus, for the victories You claim in my life and across all creation because of this name, the Lord of lords, and what it means. You hold the power and authority to bring about whatever You wish, whenever You wish it. As Revelation 17:14 says, "These [kings] will wage war against the Lamb, and the Lamb will overcome them, because He is Lord of lords and King of kings, and those who are with Him are the called and chosen and faithful." Thank You for calling me and choosing me according to Your tender mercy and care so that I may witness Your overpowering strength when You overcome all who wage war against You—and against me.

Supplication

Jesus, I want to access the power and authority You give me while on earth, which is found in the manifestation of Your name as Lord of lords. I want to overcome the enemy's attacks on my life, mind, and devotion and service to You. Give me wisdom on how to gain access to Your rule over that which seeks to bring me down and sideline me from the King's front line of service. Embolden me with the confidence that comes through knowing I have been chosen and called by You. In this way I can stand firmly against the schemes of the devil and wage victorious warfare according to all the power and might present within You, Jesus, the Lord of lords and ruler of my life.

26

MESSIAH

*You are to know and discern that from the
issuing of a decree to restore and rebuild
Jerusalem until Messiah the Prince
there will be seven weeks and sixty-two weeks;
it will be built again, with plaza and moat,
even in times of distress.*

DANIEL 9:25

Adoration

Jesus, You are the Messiah about whom the prophets spoke in the Old Testament. You are the one whom all of Israel looked to arrive. As it is written in John 1:41, "[Andrew] found first his own brother Simon and said to him, 'We have found the Messiah' (which translated means Christ)." The joy You brought to so many when they realized You are the promised Messiah resonated throughout the land and has left its impact to this day. I worship You, for You have fulfilled all that was written about You. You came that God's promise of redemption for all humanity would be made manifest to us all.

Confession

Jesus, the woman at the well who spoke with You and gave You something to drink did not immediately recognize You for who You were. In John 4:25, she said, "I know that Messiah is coming (He who is called Christ); when that One comes, He will declare all things to us." But You were the one she was speaking of. You revealed Yourself to her at that time—but Lord, I confess I am guilty of not recognizing the glory of Your purpose and the promises of Your name as well. Help me not grow complacent in my relationship with You. When I stand before You, as the woman at the well did, I want to recognize You for who You are.

Thanksgiving

Jesus, thank You for bringing about the fruition of God's promised redemption as the one who had to come in order to take away the sins of the world. Thank You for the grace that became available to us as You lived out this name for all to benefit from. Thank You that You have grafted me into Your promised people, a people chosen by You in order to do good works in Your name and bring God glory while advancing His kingdom agenda on earth. Every day that I am able to serve You and share Your love with others is a gift. Thank You for allowing me to experience life to the fullest.

Supplication

Jesus, the name Messiah literally means "the anointed one." It refers to the chosen one, called for a specific purpose and given the power to carry out that purpose from God Himself. You are the anointed one whose purpose is to bring redemption to humanity. Help me better proclaim this name of Yours to those who do not yet know You. Raise up an army of believers who will spread Your name to all who need to hear it. May I be used by You to prepare as many people as possible to happily experience Your reign as Messiah over all. May our spirits be in alignment with You so that we can worship You as You deserve.

27

MIGHTY ONE

*You will also suck the milk of nations and suck the breast
of kings; then you will know that I, the Lord, am your
Savior and your Redeemer, the Mighty One of Jacob.*

ISAIAH 60:16

Adoration

Jesus, You are the mighty one of Jacob, my Savior and redeemer.
Your might empowers all You do. It keeps the enemy at bay. It defeats
oppressors. It strips Satan of his fangs. As You said in Isaiah 49:26, "I
will feed your oppressors with their own flesh, and they will become
drunk with their own blood as with sweet wine; and all flesh will
know that I, the Lord, am your Savior and your Redeemer, the
Mighty One of Jacob." You are a gentle, loving Savior, but You are
also a mighty God against whom no one can contend and win. I worship You, for You are a warrior like none other.

Confession

Jesus, I confess that I often seek to fight my own battles when I
forget that You are the mighty one who can topple kingdoms on my
behalf. Rather than call on Your name, I throw my own punches.
They land flat, Lord, because the enemy is a stronger warrior than I

am. But You can defeat the enemy for me because You are the mighty one, my Savior and redeemer. Please forgive me for failing to hand off the ball to You when I should and trying instead to go it alone.

Thanksgiving

Jesus, thank You for all the wonderful things You have done for me. Thank You for every door You have opened for me. Thank You for giving me the ability to learn, grow, develop, mature, forgive, and move on. All of this is because of Your strong arm. It is not by my might nor my strength that I have come as far as I have. It is by Your Spirit present in this name which embodies Your strength. As Luke 1:49 says, "The Mighty One has done great things for me; and holy is His name." Yes, the mighty one has done great things for me. Holy is Your name.

Supplication

Jesus, I ask that You show up against that which is seeking to take me down. I ask that you grab Your weapons of warfare and defeat the enemy on my behalf. Give me the strength I need to call on You in times of trouble and to trust in Your great name. As Genesis 49:24 says, "His bow remained firm, and his arms were agile, from the hands of the Mighty One of Jacob (from there is the Shepherd, the Stone of Israel)." You are agile, strong, great, and mighty. I ask for Your intervention in the specific challenge I am facing right now, and I ask that You overpower it on my behalf. Show me the way to victory as I trust in You, the mighty one.

28

Morning Star

I, Jesus, have sent My angel to testify to you these things for the churches. I am the root and the descendant of David, the bright morning star.

REVELATION 22:16

Adoration

Jesus, I adore You and praise this name of Yours, O bright morning star. You are the root and descendant of David. You have sent Your angels to testify of Your power and might. May we have ears to hear and receive this name of Yours. In this name, we discover our light. We discover the guiding presence You provide. We uncover the illumination of Your wisdom and the direction of Your Word. I honor You for Your wisdom, truth, and guidance, which I depend on each moment of my day. I worship You for the way You seek to make known to each of us the fullness of this great name.

Confession

Jesus, I wonder how different my life would look if I truly set You as the morning star of my heart and mind. How much wiser my choices would be if I depended upon Your leading rather than my own. Will You be patient with me and extend a greater grace as I turn from the way of my own wisdom? Will You gently lead me toward Your light so that I can have a compass of compassion, kindness, and love in my life? You are the guide, O bright morning star. You are the hope of my calling. Help me when I fail and fall short to repent and return to You, Jesus, my morning star.

Thanksgiving

Jesus, thank You that You are a lamp shining in a dark place. Thank You that I am not left to my own ways and given over to fear in dark places. You provide the light for me to follow. You lift my head when I am afraid to look up. You are the morning star who encourages me to keep going, knowing that a new day is on the horizon. As 2 Peter 1:19 says, "We have the prophetic word made more sure, to which you do well to pay attention as to a lamp shining in a dark place, until the day dawns and the morning star arises in your hearts." Thank You for the prophetic word made sure in You, the morning star arising in my heart.

Supplication

Jesus, I want others to know this name of Yours and to experience the blessing of living according to Your will and Your ways. Give me insight on how to share this name with those around me. Show me ways to inspire others to seek You and Your names more fully so that they will grow in their relationship with You. And keep me on the path that is guided by You, the morning star, so that I do not lose my way. In all humility and gratitude, I follow You, knowing that every step I took to get me where I am today was only taken because You lit the way.

29

SHILOH

*The scepter shall not depart from Judah, nor the ruler's
staff from between his feet, until Shiloh comes, and to him
shall be the obedience of the peoples.*

GENESIS 49:10

Adoration

Jesus, Your name Shiloh can mean "he whose it is." All things are
Yours as the Messiah and great, ruling King. In Shiloh, we find our
completion. In Shiloh, we find our peace. You are the full manifestation of the comprehensive rule of God because You came to fulfill all that was written in the law and commandments. I honor You
as the owner of all, the ruler over all, and the power within all. May
Your name Shiloh testify to Your completeness and grace to all who
have ears to hear.

Confession

Jesus, I belong to You. I am Yours. You are Shiloh, the one who
has all. Forgive me for seeking to draw my own boundary lines for
what I do with the life You have given me. Forgive me for seeking my
own direction on how I spend the time You have gifted me. Forgive
me for wanting my own way when it comes to the use of the treasures

You've placed in my care. All things belong to You, and I need Your mercy for those times when I neglect to live according to this reality and truth.

Thanksgiving

Jesus, thank You for Your power and provision. Thank You for bringing all things into being. Thank You for the comfort I find in knowing all things rest in Your loving hands. Your name is Shiloh, and I can find peace in this name because the word *shiloh* means peace. You who told the waters to be still when the storm raged— who commanded the sea to be at peace—*You* are peace, and in You I find my peace. Speak peace over my life. Speak calm into my circumstances. I thank You in advance for the peace and calm You place in my soul when I look to You, Shiloh.

Supplication

Jesus, grant me release from that which holds me hostage. Whether it is fear, dread, doubt, or pain—whatever it may be—give me freedom in order to embrace peace, love, and hope in You. Let Your name of Shiloh be evident in my heart, my tone of voice, my words, and my actions. Let Your name be reflected in all I do. Give me the comfort I need to get through my days with a bright outlook on my future. I seek Your presence and perfection in my life as You, Shiloh, rule over all.

30

ROSE OF SHARON

I am the rose of Sharon, the lily of the valleys.
SONG OF SOLOMON 2:1

Adoration

Jesus, the rose of Sharon can be symbolically attributed to You as a name, giving us insight into our relationship with You as Your bride. The rose is considered the most perfect of flowers, which describes You, the perfect one. God has set up Your relationship with us to be one of intimacy, passion, and pursuit toward each other. As the rose of Sharon, you refresh each of us with the brilliance of Your beauty. May I honor and love You as a spouse would love the other. May I give You the joy from my heart which would reflect two people in love on their wedding day, and may that joy be continual throughout my days because You are deserving of all my love.

Confession

Jesus, I want to know You more intimately in a fun, exciting, and beautiful way. Sometimes I relegate my relating to You to communication that sounds more like rote than loving reality. Forgive me for those times when I remove the passion and joy of connecting and the delight of communicating from our time spent together. Help me have more and greater experiences with You, the rose of Sharon, so I can dwell in this aspect of Your character in a more intentional way.

Thanksgiving

Jesus, as a groom brings roses to the bride for their wedding, Your life is a gift containing the purest and most perfect elements of all creation. In You lies all that creates love, joy, happiness, and mutual delight. Thank You for wanting to share in my emotions at this level. Thank You for desiring to connect with Your creation in an intimate way. Thank You for pursuing me passionately and leaving me winks as I wander throughout my days. Help me see You and recognize Your joy more fully so that I can wholly embrace it with my mind, body and spirit.

Supplication

Jesus, cause us as a church body to understand this name more completely. Cause us to look to You as the rose of Sharon, our friend and companion, our lover and purely passionate connection. Help us recognize You in the nature You have so beautifully made. The flowers attest to Your own beauty. The trees dance in the wind You supply. Open our hearts and minds to see beyond mere study or theology and into the heartbeat which motivates Your love for us. Give each of us a greater glimpse behind the veil in order to invoke smiles on our faces and a desire to seek You and know You more. Delight us according to the delights found in this name, Jesus, the rose of Sharon.

31

JESUS OF NAZARETH

The crowds were saying,
"This is the prophet Jesus,
from Nazareth in Galilee."

MATTHEW 21:11

Adoration

Nazareth was an ordinary city in the time that You called it home, Jesus. It didn't have many wealthy people. It didn't stand out from other places around it. Yet You chose this place to be part of the name You would be known by. When people introduced You, they called You "Jesus of Nazareth." They may have said it degradingly: "It's Jesus from that forsaken place that produces nothing of worth at all." Nazareth was nothing more than a nondescript dot on a map when You lived there. Perhaps the name was given to put You down. Yet You wore it well. You transformed it into something which would mean royalty, dignity, individuality, and deity. You, Jesus of Nazareth, the God who was willing to identify with the most common people in the most common place, displayed Your love to us through this valuable and beautiful name.

Confession

Jesus, the humility and passion with which You pursued a loving and saving relationship with Your chosen ones is a model for all of us who follow You. You had no issue with people calling You "Jesus of Nazareth" because Your identity was not rooted in a status, location, station in life, or public role. Jesus of Nazareth, forgive me for not behaving the same. Forgive me for looking toward possessions to define me rather than seeking my identity in You alone. Forgive my lack of confidence in who I am in You, which has me running around looking for a way to define myself or display an image of worth. The name Jesus of Nazareth ought to be my guide for how I refer to myself, knowing that my worth is entirely tied to You.

Thanksgiving

Jesus of Nazareth, thank You for coming to earth and living as a boy in the town of Nazareth. Thank You for participating in the many activities that cause life to move from day to day. You probably picked grapes, ran sheep off from nearing the area where you sat, and worked with wood. You grew hungry. You slept on a bed that most likely lacked comfort—at least, it lacked the comfort of where You came from. Thank You for clothing Yourself in everything You did which would give you the right to be called Jesus of Nazareth. You came. You stayed. You lived among us. You didn't just drop in to do what You needed to do. Thank You for Your physical presence on earth.

Supplication

Jesus of Nazareth, make my heart and spirit reflect Yours. Lead me from paths which cause me to think too highly of myself. Let me embrace the ordinary days, weeks, months, and years as a gift from You, because life itself is a gift from You. May my heart give You gratitude for the things I take for granted far too many times. The name

Jesus of Nazareth reminds me to find value in everything around me because this is where You have chosen me to be. If Nazareth is good enough for Jesus, the King of the universe which He Himself created, then where You have me is certainly good enough for me.

32

LION OF THE TRIBE OF JUDAH

One of the elders said to me, "Stop weeping; behold, the Lion that is from the tribe of Judah, the Root of David, has overcome so as to open the book and its seven seals."

REVELATION 5:5

Adoration

Jesus, You are the lion from the tribe of Judah, full of power and strength. You are the root of David, the one who has overcome all so that You are able to open the book and its seven seals. Nothing is beyond Your reach. Nothing sits outside of Your power. No opposition can defeat You. You tear to pieces that which stands in the way of the Father's perfect, divinely ordained will. May You receive the honor that is due You even now before we get to see the full revelation of this name, the lion of the tribe of Judah. May you receive the awe that this name evokes as we look to You for might, authority, strength, and defense.

Confession

Jesus, I confess to You that I consider this name at times when I think about Your return, but I don't always apply the meaning of this name to my everyday life. The same power which will usher in the millennium and Your complete and total rule is the same power available to me in every situation I currently face. Forgive me for emasculating You in my mind by failing to call on Your strength when I need it the most. Forgive me for somehow thinking that I can fight my own spiritual battles in my own strength. Forgive me for failing to call on the name of the lion of the tribe of Judah so that You can display the awesome prowess of Your abilities and power in my life.

Thanksgiving

Jesus, thank You for Your power. Thank You for Your might. Thank You for leading me. Thank You that I am not fighting *for* victory in spiritual warfare; I am fighting *from* a position of victory. Thank You that You have already secured the victory for me due to the strength of Your name as the lion of the tribe of Judah. Thank You that because of this truth, I can rest. I can let go of fear. I can release anxiety. I can breathe in the peace that results from trusting in Your power.

Supplication

Jesus, go to battle for me in the difficulties I am facing. Will you crush the enemy who is seeking to bring me harm? Will you overturn the situations I cannot overturn on my own? Will you roar with the might You possess as the lion of the tribe of Judah, letting the enemy know he is not welcome in my domain? Use Your power to establish order and rule in the areas of my influence so that others may come to see Your mighty hand and the results of Your intervening strength.

33

Man of Sorrows

He was despised and forsaken of men,
a man of sorrows and acquainted with grief;
and like one from whom men hide their face
He was despised, and we did not esteem Him.

Adoration

Jesus, Your name as the man of sorrows holds within it so much more than an identification with sorrow or the revelation of the suffering You went through in pursuit of our salvation. Within this name there is a firm commitment to the Father's will because You had asked that this cup be allowed to pass from You. This is not a sorrow You sought on Your own. It is a sorrow You endured as an act of love to the Father because through Your pain on the cross, we were given the pathway to God the Father for eternal life. I praise You and worship You for Your commitment to the Father and Your love for Him, which gave You the sheer will to push through the sorrow of all sorrows in order to bring humanity the greatest gift we could ever know.

Confession

Jesus, Your sorrow ran deeper than the pain You felt or the agony

You experienced from the physical torture of the beatings and the cross. Your sorrow was rooted in the separation You experienced on my behalf as God the Father turned His back on You, and You were no longer one with Him in that moment in time. That agonizing sorrow is more than I can comprehend. Forgive me for failing to thank You for the suffering You endured emotionally, spiritually, and physically so that I would never have to be separated from God when I place my faith in You for the salvation of my sins.

Thanksgiving

Thank You, Jesus, man of sorrows, for bearing the burden of the sins of the world. All of humanity's sins were placed on You in that moment of time on the cross, and You identified with the depth of depravity which wages war with us on a daily basis. Thank You for going to so great a length in order to provide us a way out from the destruction and death which are natural consequences of sin. Thank You, Jesus, for the sorrow You felt so that we could feel joy, peace, and happiness. Thank You for loving the Father that much to provide this pathway and for loving us that much to save us.

Supplication

Jesus, help me not belittle the pain You endured as the man of sorrows by continuing to hold fast to the guilt and shame which You died to rid me of. Help me not dismiss the finality of what cost You everything. Rather, help me accept the love You freely give. Also, help me not judge others who are equally as forgiven as I am. Help me point them to the freedom Your truth provides in knowing that Your sorrow has removed our own and wiped away our shame, our guilt, and the burden of the spiritual consequences of sin upon our repentance.

34

SON OF GOD

He remained there until the death of Herod.
This was to fulfill what had been spoken
by the Lord through the prophet:
"Out of Egypt I called My Son."

MATTHEW 2:15

Adoration

Jesus, this name identifies Your relationship with God the Father. You are the Son of God and one with Him in nature. He is in You, and You reflected Him to us in such a way while You were on earth that allowed us to see Him. Through You we have understanding and knowledge of God that we did not have before You came. First John 5:20 explains it this way: "We know that the Son of God has come, and has given us understanding so that we may know Him who is true; and we are in Him who is true, in His Son Jesus Christ. This is the true God and eternal life." You are the life of God made manifest in order that we can be granted the mercy and grace we need to spend eternity with You in heaven. I praise You for Your power that shows up in this name, Son of God.

Confession

Jesus, when the disciples saw Your power up close and in person, they knew who You were. As it is written in Matthew 14:33, "Those who were in the boat worshiped Him, saying, 'You are certainly God's Son!'" They recognized You by the works You performed which showed Your power over Your creation. You calmed the sea. You caused the nets to be full of fish. You raised the dead. Yet even though I have also experienced Your great and mighty hand in my life, I sometimes fail to honor You as the Son of God. I set You on the shelf of my heart rather than recognize Your preeminence over all. Please forgive me for failing to show You the love and gratitude that is due You as the Son of God.

Thanksgiving

Jesus, salvation comes through You alone. I am gifted with eternal life by believing in Your name and what that name represents—the free gift of God for salvation due to Your sacrifice for my sins. This is only possible because You are the sinless Son of God. Thank You, Son of God, for calling me to salvation and providing the way to be saved. As John 20:31 says, "These have been written so that you may believe that Jesus is the Christ, the Son of God; and that believing you may have life in His name." Thank You for the life I have in Your name. Thank You for the life that others also have in Your name.

Supplication

Jesus, give me a stronger passion for telling others about the life they can receive through Your name, the Son of God. Give me greater boldness to share the gospel of salvation with anyone and everyone who needs to hear it. Raise up an army of evangelists whose mission it is to see Your name spread near and far so that people may believe and receive the free gift of eternal life through Your sacrifice on the cross. Bring Yourself glory through empowering me and others to spread the good news of Your great name, Son of God.

35

WORD

In the beginning was the Word,
and the Word was with God,
and the Word was God.

JOHN 1:1

Adoration

Jesus, You are the Word. In You abides every syllable and word in Scripture. You are the living Word. Through You all things were created by a word. Before any form or substance came into being, You existed as the Word. You were with God, and You were God. I worship You and honor and extol the power of this name. I give You praise for the intricate design You have created in all living things. You have caused everything to come into place and, by this name, You hold all things together. You are the source of all life, and You are the Word which produces growth, gives healing, and stops demons in their tracks.

Confession

Jesus, there is power in Scripture, Your Word. There is strength in Your Word. Abiding in You, the Word of God, gives me the ability to ask whatever I wish, and You say that You will do it. John 15:7

says, "If you abide in Me, and My words abide in you, ask what-ever you wish, and it will be done for you." The secret is in You as the Word of God—knowing You, loving You, and abiding in You. When Your words abide in me, there is nothing I cannot do. Forgive me for neglecting the great and awesome privilege of studying, med-itating on, and releasing the power of You and Your Word in my life.

Thanksgiving

Jesus, thank You for making so clear all that is needed in order to do great acts in Your name. Thank You for showing me the way to manifest Your will and glory on earth. You came as the Word, and You also left us Your Word so that we may have access to all we need in order to advance Your kingdom on earth. John 1:14 says, "The Word became flesh, and dwelt among us, and we saw His glory, glory as of the only begotten from the Father, full of grace and truth." Thank You for entrusting me with such a treasure. Thank You for entrusting all of us with this treasure. May we learn how to use Your Word more completely according to Your perfect will for our individual lives— as well as for our collective impact as a church body in this world.

Supplication

Jesus, You are the personification of both the written and spoken word of God, as demonstrated through Your life on earth. You made the Word alive in such a way that revealed the glory of God and the depth of His understanding. Show me more of You in the Word as I read through it. Give me wisdom to understand the Scriptures and apply them to my life. Give me a hunger for knowing, hearing, and telling others about the Word. Help us as a nation give greater adher-ence and honor to Your Word. May You plant within us an ongo-ing desire to meditate on Your Word and abide in You as the Word of God.

36

TRUTH

Jesus said to him, "I am the way, and the truth, and the life; no one comes to the Father but through Me."

JOHN 14:6

Adoration

Jesus, You are truth. In the day in which we live, people think there are many versions of truth. Yet there is only one truth, and You are this truth. Truth cannot be modified. Truth does not adjust to the current cultural climate or norms. Truth is rooted and founded in You. Knowing You means knowing the truth. Knowing You means knowing the way in which we are to go. Knowing You means understanding how to apply wisdom to all of life's choices. I praise You because You have made truth available to us through Your life and through this name which You came to embody so that we may see, learn from, and discover what truth really is.

Confession

Jesus, forgive me for the times when I seek answers to my questions or leading on which way to go from other sources outside of You. You are the truth, and yet I look to other people to inform my decisions. This must insult You, and I am sorry for that. I am sorry for downplaying the source of all truth by seeking other people's opinions or even by choosing my own opinion over Your wise and all-knowing truth. I ask for Your grace and mercy in helping me see the error of my ways. Correct me, Jesus, but with kindness—"lest You bring me to nothing," as Jeremiah 10:24 (NKJV) says.

Thanksgiving

Jesus, thank You for giving me the truth through Your own existence and presence on earth. Thank You for giving me the opportunity to know which way to go, even if I don't always choose it. Thank You for the patience You show when I stray from Your truth. Thank You for the restraint You show when I seek other sources of direction outside of You, even as You gently pull me back to Your Word and truth. As John 1:17 says, "The Law was given through Moses; grace and truth were realized through Jesus Christ." Thank You for the grace and truth You have made available to me so that I may live the abundant life You have promised me in Your name.

Supplication

Jesus, not only are You the Word, but You are also the sum total of that Word, which is truth. Your name is truth. And because of You, I am able to be sanctified. As John 17:17 says, "Sanctify them in the truth; Your word is truth." Help me abide more closely with You so that I can receive this gift of cleansing sanctification from You. Remove the hindrances and barriers I have against abiding fully in You and in Your Word, the truth. Show me the power I can access when I do abide in Your truth, and let that be an example to others so that they, too, will pursue You and the truth You are for their own lives.

37

Prince of Life

*You disowned the Holy and Righteous One and
asked for a murderer to be granted to you,
but put to death the Prince of life,
the one whom God raised from the dead,
a fact to which we are witnesses.*

Acts 3:14-15

Adoration

Jesus, You are the prince of life who was put to death in order that God might raise You from the dead. Through Your death, burial, and resurrection, we are each given the opportunity to trust in You for eternal life. It is in Your name that life exists. It is through Your act of sacrificial love that eternal life is offered. I worship You, for You have the power to lay down Your life and take it up again. I worship You, for by Your very word You can speak life into that which is dead and have it be raised again. In Your life is found healing, peace, grace, unconditional love, understanding, and warmth. I honor You as the prince of life because You are the source of life itself.

Confession

Jesus, taking life for granted is one of the most foolish things I have ever done. And yet I do it far more often than I even want to admit. Taking You for granted is even worse. You are my life. You are the sum total of my life. You are the meaning of my life. My identity is found in You, the prince of life. Forgive me for seeking life in other sources. Forgive me for denying You the honor and gratitude You deserve. Help me live my life according to the direction and truth found in Galatians 2:20: "I have been crucified with Christ; and it is no longer I who live, but Christ lives in me; and the life which I now live in the flesh I live by faith in the Son of God, who loved me and gave Himself up for me."

Thanksgiving

Thank You, Jesus, for every day that You give me life. Thank You for being the prince of life and the source of my life. Thank You for allowing me another day to know You and serve You. You have placed so many things on earth for us to enjoy—things created by You, like nature and animals and one another. Thank You for the joy that life provides and for encouraging me to live life to the fullest because of the abundant life You supply. Thank You for honoring me and blessing me with the gift of life. Thank You for taking joy in my praise, gratitude, and experience of life in You.

Supplication

Jesus, prince of life, show me how to maximize the life You have given me so that I can expand the reach of Your glory while advancing Your kingdom on earth. As the psalmist prayed in Psalm 90:17, "Let the favor of the Lord our God be upon us; and confirm for us the work of our hands; yes, confirm the work of our hands." Lord, life is a gift, but it has been given to me for a reason. I have a divine assignment You want me to carry out. Please give me wisdom on what this is so that my life will bring You the greatest glory and pleasure.

38

MEDIATOR

There is one God, and one mediator
also between God and men,
the man Christ Jesus.

1 TIMOTHY 2:5

Adoration

Jesus, 1 Timothy 2:5 makes this name of Yours clear for us. You are the mediator, the go-between who allows humanity to enter into God's holy presence because of Your shed blood. I praise and honor You for Your sacrifice, which provided the way to enter heaven. As Hebrews 9:15 says, "He is the mediator of a new covenant, so that, since a death has taken place for the redemption of the transgressions that were committed under the first covenant, those who have been called may receive the promise of the eternal inheritance." I praise You for the promise of the eternal inheritance which You have supplied through the power of this mighty name.

Confession

Jesus, humanity has needed You and the manifestation of this name of Yours as mediator since the beginning of time. Since the first sin in the garden which led to a continual presence of sin in the nature of mankind, we have been removed from the presence of God. Our relationship with the Father was severed by sin. But as Hebrews 12:22,24 says, "You have come…to Jesus, the mediator of a new covenant, and to the sprinkled blood, which speaks better than the blood of Abel." You have created and gifted us a new covenant. Forgive me for my sins which caused my initial separation from God. Forgive me for my sins which made the cross a reality and need. Forgive me for my sins which You felt, paid for, and removed through Your righteous atonement.

Thanksgiving

Jesus, thank You for the vast number of promises which appear in Your holy Word. Thank You for the truth of these promises. You have given us access to these promises by Your role as mediator. Thank You for Your ministry, which has created a better covenant based on the promise of eternal life. As Hebrews 8:6 says, "Now He has obtained a more excellent ministry, by as much as He is also the mediator of a better covenant, which has been enacted on better promises." Thank You for standing in the gap between myself and God the Father, giving me the bridge to cross over that gap and into His loving arms. Thank You for rescuing me from eternal separation and torment so that I can live forever in the warmth of God's unconditional love, which has been freely given through Your sacrifice for my sins as the mediator.

Supplication

Jesus, help others come to a saving knowledge of You through this name of Yours as the mediator between humanity and God's presence. Send workers into the fields in order to reap a harvest of souls. Jesus, raise up a group of people who will make evangelizing others their life mission and goal. Draw all men to Yourself so that they can benefit from Your mediation on their behalf. Give me wisdom and insight on how I can influence others toward salvation in You within the realms of my personal stewardship. Show me how You want me to use my time, talents, and treasures to point people to You, the only mediator between a holy God and sinful humanity.

39

SAVIOR

*Today in the city of David there has been born for you a
Savior, who is Christ the Lord.*

LUKE 2:11

Adoration

Jesus, Your name Savior contains the gift of eternal life. You are
the chosen one who has brought a way for me to enter into the promises of God. The life You provide is for eternity, but it is also to be
experienced in time by accessing God through prayer with boldness.
I adore You for Your power. I praise the Father for sending You as the
Savior. As Acts 13:23 says of You, "According to promise, God has
brought to Israel a Savior, Jesus." Receive my highest honor given
from the deepest level of humility because without You as the Savior, I could not even pray right now. I would not be heard. I worship
You for looking down from on high and having mercy and compassion on Your creation at such a level that You were willing to offer
Yourself as Savior.

Confession

Jesus, Scripture tells us plainly that this name, Savior, is the revelation of our passageway to heaven. It is through You and You alone.

Acts 4:12 says, "There is salvation in no one else; for there is no other name under heaven that has been given among men by which we must be saved." You provide the way. It doesn't come through being good. It doesn't come through avoiding bad. Eternal life comes through placing my faith in You alone as my Savior. You are the Savior of the world. Forgive us as Your creation for having concocted so many false ways to go to heaven. Have mercy on our hearts.

Thanksgiving

Jesus, thank You that one day You will return and bring Your glory in its fullest form of manifestation to this earth. Thank You for the grace of Your return. Thank You for letting us know that You will one day return. As Titus 2:13 says, we are "looking for the blessed hope and the appearing of the glory of our great God and Savior, Christ Jesus." Thank You for loving us so much that You want to be near us. You are a compassionate, personal, relational Savior.

Supplication

Jesus, 1 John 4:14 reminds me that You did not just come to save me or to save my family and friends, but You came to save the entire world. It says, "We have seen and testify that the Father has sent the Son to be the Savior of the world." Show me how You want me to reach more people for You in order to tell them about You as the Savior. Place ideas in my mind and in the church collectively as Your body so that we may be used as instruments which proclaim Your name as Savior to as many people as possible. Give me wisdom on how to share Your name with others in every way You desire me to do so.

40

MIGHTY GOD

A child will be born to us, a son will be given to us;
and the government will rest on His shoulders;
and His name will be called Wonderful Counselor,
Mighty God, Eternal Father,
Prince of Peace.

ISAIAH 9:6

Adoration

Jesus, the name Mighty God speaks to Your power and strength. It speaks to Your rule as King. It speaks to Your glory as the Almighty. I worship You for who You are, lifting up my heart to praise Your might. I praise You for Your ability to help me overcome anything with which the enemy seeks to destroy me. I worship You for the grace You show me time and time again. I honor Your strength. You are a warrior unlike any other. You merely speak the word, and the opposition runs away. May Your name Mighty God resonate within my soul in such a strong way that I feel Your confidence. May fear and doubt be banished from my heart by knowing the truth of this name.

Confession

Jesus, You are the Mighty God who gives me all I need to be set free from emotional, spiritual, and mental bondage. I confess that I stay bound longer than I should because of a refusal to apply the truth of this name to my every situation. You have made it clear that I am to cast down any thought that is in opposition to Your truth, yet rather than cast down those thoughts, I oftentimes meditate on them. I let them sit, soak, and sour. Jesus, may Your name Mighty God echo throughout my soul so loudly that I am unable to ponder the lies the enemy has caused me to believe. In Your forgiveness, give me mercy.

Thanksgiving

Jesus, thank You for Your name Mighty God. You are the sacrifice who, like a sheep being led to slaughter, did not even open Your mouth to resist. Even though You could have called thousands of angels to defeat the scheme set against You, You exhibited the greatest amount of might and strength in resisting the ability to do so. Your sacrifice on the cross is the single greatest display of Your power and might. The nails could not hold You to the cross. You held Yourself there. Thank You for expressing Your might in such a beautiful, empowering, and loving way.

Supplication

Jesus, I need Your might to show up more often in my life. Help me incorporate this name of Yours, Mighty God, more frequently into my thoughts and prayers. Help me rest, knowing You are in control. Give me wisdom on how to access this name of Yours and the strength You are willing to give me through it. Defeat the enemy through this name, Jesus. Overcome the opposition through Your might. Surround me with Your protection, peace, and power so that I can let go of worry, anxiety, and fear. I seek You, wanting the meaning of this name, Mighty God, to be made real to me on a regular basis. Let me testify of Your great and mighty works as You allow me to experience this name more intimately in my life.

41

Messenger of the Covenant

"Behold, I am going to send My messenger,
and he will clear the way before Me.
And the Lord, whom you seek, will suddenly come
to His temple; and the messenger of the covenant,
in whom you delight, behold, He is coming,"
says the Lord of hosts.

Malachi 3:1

Adoration

Jesus, You are holy. You are love. You are "the image of the invisible God," as Colossians 1:15 says. I praise You for Your willingness to come to earth to manifest the Father's presence so that we may know God more fully—and You came with many other purposes as well. One of those purposes is found in Your name as the messenger of the covenant. You brought the good news of a new covenant which is rooted and founded in Your sacrificial love. You are not only the messenger, but You are also the supplier through whom the covenant has been sealed. I worship Your wholeness and power that enable You to do and be all of this and more.

Confession

Jesus, I want to spend a moment confessing my lack of abiding in this name of Yours, messenger of the covenant. I abide in Your names which exemplify peace, provision, and power. But this name often gets overlooked by me. Forgive me for lessening its value in my heart and mind. I honor and worship You now for what You have done on my behalf through the New Covenant of Your blood.

Thanksgiving

Jesus, thank You for the message of the New Covenant, which has been brought about through Your unconditional love. Thank You for loving and valuing me so much that I have been made a recipient of God's grace and favor through this New Covenant. Let the old ways in me disappear, as it says in Hebrews 8:13: "When He said, 'A new covenant,' He has made the first obsolete. But whatever is becoming obsolete and growing old is ready to disappear." Let Your New Covenant be prominent over my sinful flesh and thoughts so that I can please You in all I do and think.

Supplication

Jesus, this New Covenant which You have come to share was brought about through Your life, death, and resurrection. In Luke 22:20 I read, "In the same way He took the cup after they had eaten, saying, 'This cup which is poured out for you is the new covenant in My blood.'" Please let me be a part of sharing the salvation which comes through the New Covenant of Your blood. Help me encourage others to know and believe in this New Covenant. Give me a great boldness in sharing the gospel with others.

42

WITNESS

Behold, I have made him a witness to the peoples,
a leader and commander for the peoples.

ISAIAH 55:4

Adoration

Jesus, You are a witness to all of us, as well as a leader and commander. You have also created nature and the elements to witness of Your great power. This witness is true, and I worship You for the way You hold all things together. I praise You for the witness You provide for the afterlife. I give You glory for the witness You provide for life after death. I have no fear when I set my heart and mind on You, the witness of all the great things God has done and is doing for those whom He loves.

Confession

Jesus, Your witness surrounds me as I go about my day. The witness of the love of God shows up when I am given mercy time and time again. Yet I somehow forget to thank You as often as I should. I get so caught up in the busyness of this life that my mind does not rest on You or acknowledge the power of Your witness in my spirit.

Forgive me for neglecting to spend more time with You by loving You throughout my day. Forgive me for failing to recognize Your witness throughout Your creation, of which Romans 1:20 states, "Since the creation of the world His invisible attributes, His eternal power and divine nature, have been clearly seen, being understood through what has been made, so that they are without excuse."

Thanksgiving

Jesus, I thank You that You have brought a witness to us of goodness, love, kindness, compassion, humility, and strength. You are the great warrior who witnesses of God's power, but does so in a way that also highlights His gentle love. Thank You for revealing Yourself in all the ways You have in order for us to continually receive a witness of Your grace and God's saving power through Your life. Thank You for paving the way and modeling the life we are all to follow. Thank You for providing the Holy Spirit, who has come to empower me to live my life according to Your will. Thank You that Your witness shows me how to be a witness, too, for God and His love for others.

Supplication

Jesus, help me be a witness like You. I want my life to radiate the love of God so that when other people see me, they cannot help but realize they have caught a glimpse of the ever-expanding and unending love of God. Let my words be a witness of Your truth. Let my actions be a witness of what faith in You looks like. Let the favor and blessings You pour out on me be a witness of the mercy that has been made available to each of us through Your sacrifice. Show me how to better use my time, talents, and treasures to live as a witness to Your kingdom values and Your great love.

43

TRUE VINE

I am the true vine, and My Father is the vinedresser.
JOHN 15:1

Adoration

Jesus, You are the life source for all I do. Fill me with Your love. Fill me with the sap of Your sacrifice so that I can produce fruit which glorifies You. You have shared why You are the true vine, and it is so that I may experience the joy of the Father's love and Your love. It says in John 15:9-11, "Just as the Father has loved Me, I have also loved you; abide in My love. If you keep My commandments, you will abide in My love; just as I have kept My Father's commandments and abide in His love. These things I have spoken to you so that My joy may be in you, and that your joy may be made full." I praise You for Your compassionate love which makes the way for my joy to be full.

Confession

Jesus, I have neglected the power You have given me as the true vine which provides me access to God through prayer. You chose me to bear fruit, and yet I often focus on my own ego and ambitions over abiding in You. As it says in John 15:16-17, "You did not choose Me but I chose you, and appointed you that you would go and bear fruit, and that your fruit would remain, so that whatever you ask of the Father in My name He may give to you. This I command you, that you love one another." Forgive me for the lack of love in my heart, because love is the fruit You desire me to bear. It is easy to love people I like, Lord, but You have asked me to love my enemies and to love those toward whom I am apathetic. Show me mercy in this lack of love when I stand before You on the day of judgment.

Thanksgiving

Jesus, thank You that I can do all things through You. As it says in John 15:5, "I am the vine, you are the branches; he who abides in Me and I in him, he bears much fruit, for apart from Me you can do nothing." Thank You for making it clear in Your Word that I can do nothing apart from You. This way, I do not have to waste my time trying to bear fruit on my own because You have already told me it won't work. Jesus, thank You for the grace which You supply in this invitation to abide. Thank You for always being present and desiring an abiding relationship with me.

Supplication

Jesus, John 15:4 says, "Abide in Me, and I in you. As the branch cannot bear fruit of itself unless it abides in the vine, so neither can you unless you abide in Me." This is my prayer. I ask for wisdom on how to abide more often with You. I ask for nudges throughout my day reminding me to abide in You. Teach me what this means to abide in You. Let me marvel at the fruit You produce when I do.

44

DOOR

Jesus said to them again, "Truly, truly, I say to you, I am the door of the sheep. All who came before Me are thieves and robbers, but the sheep did not hear them. I am the door; if anyone enters through Me, he will be saved, and will go in and out and find pasture."

JOHN 10:7-9

Adoration

Jesus, Your name as the door speaks of how You allow me to enter into the presence of God. It speaks of You standing in the gap which divides sinful humanity from a holy God. It speaks of You as the passageway between this world and the next dimension, in which we get to experience the unending knowledge and love of God. I praise You for being this door which gives me hope. I do not have to live my life in fear of the future because You have promised You are the door to glory.

Confession

Jesus, forgive me for choosing so many other doors in this existence as I've sought satisfaction, pleasure, status, and my own glory. Forgive me for knocking on other doors and pursuing other ways to my purpose, when my purpose is clearly and entirely rooted in You. Forgive me for failing to speak up to others in order to tell them that You are the door to eternal glory as well as abundant life on earth.

Thanksgiving

Jesus, thank You for how You lead me. Like a sheep who wanders and does not know the safest direction to travel, I also wander in my life. Your loving guidance always directs me back to You—the door to safety. You are the door to my purpose. You are the door to my happiness. Thank You for guiding me to You so faithfully and for providing Your peace when I rest in You. Help me enter through the door so that I may discover the joy of Your presence in every moment of my life.

Supplication

Jesus, protect me from my own ego. Protect me from my own sinful flesh. Protect me from my own mind, which tries to steer me off course. I do not know which door to go through. You have to show me which one is You. I ask for Your gentle guidance in my life so that I may find You every step of the way. The world holds many dangers, but when I abide in You as the door, I am kept safe. Show me the way to You so that I can live with the peace that comes from Your loving protection.

45

CORNERSTONE

*The stone which the builders
rejected has become the
chief corner stone.*

PSALM 118:22

Adoration

Jesus, You are the cornerstone. You are the security of the foundation itself. Without You, the foundation crumbles with wear. Without You, the foundation shifts with the passing of time. But You hold
all things in place. As is written of You in Isaiah 28:16, "Thus says
the Lord GOD, 'Behold, I am laying in Zion a stone, a tested stone, a
costly cornerstone for the foundation, firmly placed. He who believes
in it will not be disturbed.'" It is in believing in You that we have the
opportunity to live lives which are not disturbed or shaken by the circumstances surrounding us. May Your name be praised on earth as
it is in heaven.

Confession

Jesus, rejecting You means rejecting the cornerstone of life itself.
As Acts 4:11 says, "He is the stone which was rejected by you, the

builders, but which became the chief corner stone." Forgive me for rejecting You many times throughout my days when I fail to abide in You. Forgive me for lacking love in my heart, which is the embodiment of You. I ask for Your mercy—the mercy that covers all sins. Forgive me for the disunity I have contributed to in the body of Christ throughout my life, whether in words or actions, because I am a living stone whose purpose is to reflect You, the cornerstone, to others.

Thanksgiving

Jesus, thank You that You have invited me to participate with You in bringing unity and harmony to earth and humanity. As Ephesians 2:19-22 says, "You are no longer strangers and aliens, but you are fellow citizens with the saints, and are of God's household, having been built on the foundation of the apostles and prophets, Christ Jesus Himself being the corner stone, in whom the whole building, being fitted together, is growing into a holy temple in the Lord, in whom you also are being built together into a dwelling of God in the Spirit." Thank You for letting me be built on You, the cornerstone, and for giving me the high calling of being part of a dwelling of God.

Supplication

Jesus, I ask that You empower and strengthen me to build that which You desire to be made on You, the cornerstone. I have been created to contribute to the establishment of a spiritual house, wherein spiritual sacrifices of love, kindness, compassion, and mercy can be offered. As 1 Peter 2:4-5 says, "Coming to Him as to a living stone which has been rejected by men, but is choice and precious in the sight of God, you also, as living stones, are being built up as a spiritual house for a holy priesthood, to offer up spiritual sacrifices acceptable to God through Jesus Christ." I ask for greater strength and focus in order to carry out this purpose in my life. May Your name, cornerstone, be ever present in my mind so that I can remember my destiny all the more.

46

ALMIGHTY

"I am the Alpha and the Omega,"
says the Lord God, "who is and who was
and who is to come, the Almighty."

REVELATION 1:8

Adoration

Jesus, Almighty is Your name. This name reigns and rules. This name carries with it the seal of final authority. Nothing comes into being that You did not choose to come into being. Nothing reaches me without first passing through Your fingers. I glorify this great name of Yours as I mirror the heart of the angels. As recorded in Revelation 4:8, "The four living creatures, each one of them having six wings, are full of eyes around and within; and day and night they do not cease to say, 'Holy, holy, holy is the Lord God, the Almighty, who was and who is and who is to come.'" Holy, holy, holy are You, Jesus, the Almighty.

Confession

Jesus, the strength You have as the Almighty has been made available to me. In Your strength, I can win the spiritual battles with the enemy. In Your strength, I can live victoriously over my own sinful flesh and ego. Your Word says in Ephesians 6:10, "Be strong in the Lord and in the strength of His might." Yet, for some reason, I often seek to fight my battles in my own anemic strength. Forgive me for failing to tap into the power of Your name, the Almighty, when You have made it so readily available to me.

Thanksgiving

Jesus, You rule over all. Thank You for the order which comes from Your rule. Thank You for the love by which You rule. Thank You that even though You are the Lord of all, You do not remove Yourself from me. You are present with me and accessible to me at all times. Thank You for Your humble rule as the Almighty. Revelation 19:6 says, "I heard something like the voice of a great multitude and like the sound of many waters and like the sound of mighty peals of thunder, saying, 'Hallelujah! For the Lord our God, the Almighty, reigns.'" This high, powerful, and awesome rule protects me, guides me, and provides me with all I need to live the purpose You have chosen for me. Thank You.

Supplication

Jesus, show me the surpassing greatness of this name, Almighty. Give me a glimpse into the strength of Your might. As Ephesians 1:18-20 says, "I pray that the eyes of your heart may be enlightened, so that you will know...what is the surpassing greatness of His power toward us who believe. These are in accordance with the working of the strength of His might which He brought about in Christ." I ask to see Your arm and power revealed as You work miracles in my life and in the lives of those I come into contact with. Lead me into experiences which glorify Your name, Almighty. Surround me with people who also desire to live according to the surpassing greatness of Your power toward us who believe. I love You and thank You for allowing me to have this gift of life.

47

BELOVED SON

Behold, My Servant whom I have chosen;
My Beloved in whom My soul is well-pleased;
I will put My Spirit upon Him,
and He shall proclaim justice
to the Gentiles.

MATTHEW 12:18

Adoration

Jesus, only You can claim the name of the beloved Son of God. I am a child of God, and we who are the Father's children have gained access to Him through You. You are the beloved Son who carried out the divine purpose of redemption. Thank You for the glory of this name. I praise You for the high esteem this name holds within it. I worship You as the beloved Son, through whom the sacrifice of sins was made. May You receive on earth the worship that is given to You in heaven as those whom You have redeemed recognize You as the beloved Son.

Confession

Jesus, forgive me for taking Your role as the beloved Son of God for granted and not showing You the honor and value You deserve.

Forgive me for those times when, as a selfish child, I lift myself and my wants ahead of You. You modeled what true love is when You gave Your life as the beloved Son so that I could be a child of the King. I ask for Your forgiveness of my failure to reflect what You modeled to those around me.

Thanksgiving

Thank You, Jesus, for coming to earth as the beloved Son. Thank You for leaving the love, joy, and connection of heaven in order to bring the love of God to humanity. Thank You for your obedience that You learned through suffering, as Hebrews 5:8 tells me. This obedience took You to the cross when You did not, in Your flesh, want to go through that torment. But You prayed that the Father's will be done, not Your own. Thank You for showing me what it looks like to be an obedient child of God.

Supplication

Jesus, I want to love You like the Father loves You as His beloved Son. I want my love for You to be so present in my heart that it consumes my thoughts. I want Your name to flow freely from my mouth when I am speaking to others. Jesus, become my beloved as You increase my devotion to You. Show me what it means to abide in You. Communicate with me so that I am encouraged along this path of growth in knowing You. Then let me be a light in the darkness of this lost world to radiate Your love, the beloved love of the Father in You, to others.

48

AUTHOR OF SALVATION

*Having been made perfect, He became to all those who
obey Him the source of eternal salvation.*

HEBREWS 5:9

Adoration

I praise You, Jesus, for being the source—the author—of salvation. I honor You with all that is within me because without salvation, I would be destined to eternal separation from God. In that separation is great pain, agony, regret, remorse, and torture. You, as the author of my salvation, have given me the way to escape hell. I praise and worship You for providing the bridge to heaven through Your very life. Receive my highest honor and glory as I look to You, Jesus, the author of my salvation. All praise is Yours, whether on earth or in the heavens. All worship belongs to You. If we did not worship You, the rocks and grass and trees and flowers would cry out to You, because You deserve the praise and honor of that which You have created.

Confession

Jesus, forgive me for falling short of the glory of God. Forgive me for failing to spread the good news of Your name as the author of our salvation to as many people as I can. Forgive me for forgetting this name and not mentioning it to those who need to hear it and be saved by You. Jesus, forgive all of us in Your body who focus so much on building buildings or creating personal platforms, rather than using our lives to spread the gospel as much as possible. Jesus, remind me that this life isn't about status or money. It is about spreading the good news of salvation so that souls can be rescued from an eternal destiny spent in hell.

Thanksgiving

Jesus, thank You for saving me. Thank You for authoring my salvation. Thank You for bringing into existence a way by which I can be saved. Thank You for snatching me from the pit of flames and eternal torment. Thank You for showing me what true love is—laying down one's life for another. Thank You for bearing the sins of all humanity through Your death on the cross. Thank You for paying the price of redemption. Thank You for giving me a reason to hope.

Supplication

Jesus, make my words honoring and pleasing to You as the author of our salvation. Give me courage to share the gospel with others. Reveal to me the steps I am to take which will increase my ability to demonstrate Your love to others and draw them to You for Your saving grace. I want to honor this name of Yours by living a holy life. Help me feel Your pleasure in what I do. Help me identify the purpose You have for me. Give me wisdom and insight as I go about my days in order to make the most of each opportunity so that it is used for Your glory and for sharing the truth about the author of our salvation.

49

DELIVERER

All Israel will be saved; just as it is written,
"The Deliverer will come from Zion,
He will remove ungodliness from Jacob."

ROMANS 11:26

Adoration

Jesus, I praise You for relieving me of the consequences of sin. I honor You as the deliverer of souls. Your great name as the deliverer gives insight into Your saving power. Receive my heart's praise. Enjoy my worship that I give You. Cause me to worship You more than I already do. Grow my love for You so deep that I am in an ongoing state of praise for who You are as the deliverer of my soul. To be bound to sin and oppressed by the enemy is the worst experience a person can have. Thank You for being the deliverer who has set me free.

Confession

Jesus, Your name declares that I am free. Your name makes it known that none of us have to be chained to Satan's lies or fall victim to his schemes. You are the deliverer who has opened the door to a life of abundance, peace, and love. Forgive me when I dwell in the darkness of that which I no longer need to abide in. Forgive me when I allow wrong thoughts of hate, revenge, or jealousy to dominate my mind. Forgive me for not always living freely in the deliverance You have supplied.

Thanksgiving

Thank You, Jesus, that I am no longer a slave to sin. Thank You that Satan cannot have dominion over me because You have delivered me from his grip. Thank You for delivering me from my own propensities toward envy, pride, and self-righteousness. I am full of gratitude for Your delivering power. Let my life be a testament of gratitude to those around me as I bask in Your gifts of love, compassion, hope, and joy. Thank You for using pain to teach me these lessons and for using trials to teach me obedience to You, my deliverer.

Supplication

Jesus, open my eyes to see the deliverance You died to provide. Open my eyes to recognize all the gifts You are offering me through Your deliverance—gifts of peace, love, and acceptance. Your love is greater than anything I know, and yet I've only tasted a portion of it. Will You give me a greater taste? Will You make Your presence so manifested in my soul that I cannot deny the delivering power of who You are? Bless me, Jesus, with the freedom that comes from Your deliverance. And give me the wisdom of restraint when my sinful heart starts to judge someone else. They have also been offered deliverance by You, Jesus, and are loved by You. Help me point them toward Your love rather than ridicule them for their current state of being.

50

Righteous One

*Which one of the prophets did
your fathers not persecute?
They killed those who had previously
announced the coming
of the Righteous One,
whose betrayers and murderers
you have now become.*

Acts 7:52

Adoration

Jesus, we are called to seek the kingdom of God and the righteousness of this kingdom, as it says in Matthew 6:33. You are the righteous one. You are the full manifestation of this righteousness. In seeking righteousness, we are literally seeking You. I look to You with a heart full of love because of Your purity and goodness. I lift Your name in honor. You are high above all else, seated in the heavenly realm as the righteous one. Every decision of Yours is just. Every thought of Yours is righteous. You work all things together for good because in You there is no evil. In You there is no sin. In You is the light of life itself.

Confession

Jesus, I come before You on behalf of our nation regarding the sins we have committed. We have neglected to care for the environment, Your creation, in a manner which is honoring to You. We use it without thought of the future. We contaminate it without realizing we are polluting Your perfect plan for us. We treat one another with contempt, anger, and strife, and we even murder—often the most innocent of us all, the lives of unborn souls. Jesus, forgive us for the sins of our nation as we are all collectively responsible before You, the righteous one.

Thanksgiving

Thank You, Jesus, for Your righteousness. Thank You for giving us an example of focusing on what truly matters in life. Scripture speaks of what it means to be righteous, and that is to live a life abiding in You and Your Word. As Colossians 3:12 says, "As those who have been chosen of God, holy and beloved, put on a heart of compassion, kindness, humility, gentleness and patience." The holiness spoken of in this passage reflects You as the righteous one. Thank You for showing us exactly what it means to live righteously. We are to be compassionate, kind, humble, gentle, and patient. We are to love like You have loved.

Supplication

Jesus, refine me according to Your name, righteous one. Take away that which is in opposition to Your righteousness. Grow that which reflects it. May I be patient, kind, loving, and compassionate—especially to those who make life difficult for me. Remove distractions from my life which keep me from abiding in and reflecting Your righteousness to others. Convict me when I am wasting my time. Convict me when I am sinning. Direct my thoughts toward

Your righteousness and help me dwell on You and Your love more often. Let Your righteousness come through me to others, bringing them the compassion and love they need in order to grow in their relationship with You and desire for You.

51

LAWGIVER

The LORD is our judge, the LORD is our lawgiver,
the LORD is our king; He will save us.
ISAIAH 33:22

Adoration

Jesus, You are the judge, but You are also the lawgiver. Your name identifies Your role in establishing the laws by which we are to live. At the beginning of time, You gave a number of laws. But when You came in the flesh, You said that You fulfilled these laws through Your life, death, and resurrection. Now we are to live under the two great commandments—which are to love God with all our hearts and to love others as ourselves. These are the laws which govern our lives. I praise You for simplifying what we need to know and do so that we can truly understand Your expectations for us. We are without excuse when it comes to the law because You have made it clear as the lawgiver.

Confession

Jesus, following rules and regulations is often easier than following the two overarching laws You have given us—that of loving God and loving others. Loving sounds easy, but authentic love is an emptying of oneself for the betterment of others, and that is anything but easy. I confess my selfishness to You. I repent of my sin of pride. I ask for Your forgiveness for failing to love those whom I have yet to even forgive. You have said we are to forgive as God has forgiven us. To do any less is to violate the law of love which You have established as the great lawgiver.

Thanksgiving

Thank You, Jesus, for giving me clear insight into Your expectations for my life. Thank You for blessing me with clarity. Thank You that I do not need to guess about what You want from me. You want me to love God with all my heart and to love others with the kind of love that You have given me. This accepting, unconditional, forgiving, nonjudgmental love is the sort of love that I am to show to others in my thoughts and actions. To do any less is to dishonor You and to discredit the love You have made available to me. Help me help others see and recognize their value in Your eyes. Help me point them to Your affirming, welcoming love.

Supplication

Jesus, I want to stand before You when I get to heaven and hear that You are pleased. I want You to smile and say that I truly did love You and others as You had hoped I would and had created me to do. Gently nudge me when I am moving away from this love in my life. Nudge me back to embracing Your love and spreading it to others. This is Your highest law—loving God and others. You are the great lawgiver, and I cannot argue with what You have determined is the bar against which I will be judged. Instead, I must aim to do what You desire, and that is to love You wholly, completely, and with gratitude, as well as to love others unconditionally.

52

LEADER AND COMMANDER

*Behold, I have made him a witness to the peoples, a leader
and commander for the peoples.*

Isaiah 55:4

Adoration

Jesus, You are the leader and commander over all. At times it
looks like someone or something else is leading this world, with all
the chaos and confusion, but that is because You have given us free
will in this life. Satan has power, but he does not have authority. His
power produces strife in this world, but we can appeal to Your authority to overcome him. Thank You for leading us and commanding us
with such grace. I praise You for Your might, power, authority, and
wisdom.

Confession

Jesus, my desire is to follow Your lead and command in my life,
but I don't always do that. I try to fight my own battles. I do it all
the time—You know I do. And when I do, I have to learn this lesson
again, the lesson of surrendering to Your lead and command. Forgive
me for my pride. It is pride which goes against this name of Yours.

Forgive me for allowing my pride to trip me up from the call of loving others, serving them, and surrendering to Your overarching rule in my life.

Thanksgiving

Jesus, thank You for Your command over all. When the disciples were in the storm on the Sea of Galilee, You calmed their fears by calming the sea. Thank You that one word from Your mouth is enough to settle the storms in life. Thank You that I can rest knowing that You are in control. My heart is full of gratitude for Your leading and Your command in the circumstances that seek to tear me down. Show me what it means to know this name of Yours more fully. I give You thanks ahead of time for what You are about to reveal to me. With You as the leader and commander, I have no fear.

Supplication

Jesus, lead me. Create in me such a pure heart that I follow Your lead. You are the commander not only of all creation and all creatures, but also of my mind, thoughts, and hopes. Let me align myself under Your command. Then, when I do, show up for me in those battles that I had previously sought to wage on my own. Show me Your great command as You silence my enemies and remove my oppressors. Show me Your command as You reverse the scenarios of life that are situated against me. Command my worry, anxiety, and fear to stop. Command peace to enter my heart. Command love and joy to permeate my existence, so that I find significance in loving and knowing You.

53

Son of the Blessed One

He kept silent and did not answer.
Again the high priest was questioning Him,
and saying to Him, "Are You the Christ,
the Son of the Blessed One?"
And Jesus said, "I am."

Mark 14:61-62

Adoration

Jesus, You are the Son of the blessed one. Your name reveals Your willingness to enter a woman's womb and this world's dimension. You name reveals Your purpose, which was to come to earth as the Christ, the Messiah, in order to redeem us from the penalty of sin. I praise and worship You for Your great name. I lift up Your name, Son of the blessed one, with a heart full of gratitude and hope.

Confession

Jesus, because You came to earth and provided deliverance from sin, I am able to approach God's throne with boldness and courage. As the Son of the blessed one, You made this possible. You took on flesh so that I could discover what it means to abide in the Spirit and to let the Spirit grow me. I confess that I often focus on the material things of this world rather than on feeding and nurturing the seed of faith planted in me through Your willingness to come as the Son of the blessed one. Forgive me for my many distractions that draw me away from You.

Thanksgiving

Thank You, Jesus, for blessing each of us by coming to us as the Son of the blessed one. Thank You for choosing to enter the world in such an obscure way to such unknown people so that You could manifest the Father's love to us all. You are one with God the Father, and yet You are also the Son. You are the same in essence with Him as a member of the Trinity, yet You willingly chose to be named Son of the blessed one. Your humility gives me the ability to surrender to the hierarchy that You have allowed me to be placed within as well. I can learn from You in this manner. Thank You for modeling obedience through being one with God, yet obeying the Father as His Son, even to the point of death.

Supplication

Jesus, I need to have a heart of service that more closely mirrors Yours. As the Son of the blessed one, You gave Your life to do the Father's will. I want to give my life to do His will too. I ask that You show me how to do that on a more regular basis. Nudge me when I am chasing after empty pursuits. Help me realize when my heart is being consumed by anything other than what comprises Your nature—which is love, compassion, grace, and mercy. Mold me into Your likeness, Jesus—for though You are equal with God, You counted serving the Father Your highest honor as the Son of the blessed one. I want to be like You, Jesus. Make me into Your image so that others can see You in me.

54

TRUE LIGHT

There was the true Light which,
coming into the world,
enlightens every man.

JOHN 1:9

Adoration

Jesus, You are the true light. Your light enlightens all who look
to You to receive it. Without You, we are lost in utter darkness. You
are the light of the world. As it is written in John 8:12, "Jesus again
spoke to them, saying, 'I am the Light of the world; he who follows
Me will not walk in the darkness, but will have the Light of life.'" I
praise You for Your light. Bask in the worship of my heart as I bask in
the warm light of Your presence. You provide the way for each of us
to walk because You illuminate the path before us. Receive the honor
that is due You as the light which gives insight, hope, love, and salvation to all.

Confession

Jesus, many sleep without knowing Your light. Many die without
coming to the one who gives life. As it says in Ephesians 5:14, "Awake,
sleeper, and arise from the dead, and Christ will shine on you." Not

everyone comes to know Your light or receives the salvation which You died to give them. Forgive me for not using the life You've given me to call out to others so that they will awake for You to shine on them. Forgive me for wasting so much of my time, talents, and treasures, with little regard to the lost all around me. May those souls who are living without Your life have the benefit of coming to know You, Jesus, as the true light You are.

Thanksgiving

Jesus, thank You for coming to this world so that we may know the true light. As You said in John 9:5, "While I am in the world, I am the Light of the world." You remained on the earth as a witness and testimony to the light You give and supply. And when You returned to heaven, You sent the Holy Spirit to testify concerning this light, as well, and to convict us when we walk away from the light. Thank You for the loving light You provide. Thank You for showing me which way to go on my journey toward knowing You more. Thank You for illuminating the sin in my heart so that I can confess and repent of it right away. I give You the gratitude of my heart for Your light.

Supplication

Jesus, You are the light of the world who came so that those whom You save may then become lights and share of Your love with others. As Philippians 2:14-15 says, "Do all things without grumbling or disputing; so that you will prove yourselves to be blameless and innocent, children of God above reproach in the midst of a crooked and perverse generation, among whom you appear as lights in the world." Make me shine with Your light and send Your light all around me. This starts with me living above reproach in the midst of this crooked and perverse generation. Radiate my light in such a way that it draws people to You, the true light, so that they may experience for themselves Your forgiving, compassionate love.

55

PRINCE OF PEACE

A child will be born to us,
a son will be given to us;
and the government will rest on His shoulders;
and His name will be called
Wonderful Counselor, Mighty God,
Eternal Father, Prince of Peace.

ISAIAH 9:6

Adoration

Jesus, the name Prince of Peace means that You Yourself are the embodiment of peace. Not only that, but You rule over all manifestations of peace. When You speak peace, peace comes about. When You command peace, peace responds. You tell peace where to go and where to reside. Your peace passes all understanding. It is beyond figuring out. You are the peace in the midst of crises and emergencies. Your peace guards hearts and minds. As John 14:27 says, "Peace I leave with you; My peace I give to you; not as the world gives do I give to you. Do not let your heart be troubled, nor let it be fearful." Fear has no place in my heart because You are the Prince of Peace, whom I worship.

Confession

Jesus, all I need to do in order to be free from worry, anxiety, and fear is to obey Scripture, which states in Colossians 3:15, "Let the peace of Christ rule in your hearts, to which indeed you were called in one body; and be thankful." It's as simple as that. When Your peace rules in my heart, I can have no more fear, doubt, or dread. Forgive me for resisting Your peace. Forgive me for putting a barrier around my heart which keeps Your peace from ruling over me. I invite Your peace to rule my heart, Lord Jesus, as I confess my sins to You.

Thanksgiving

Jesus, Your name Prince of Peace can accomplish so many wonderful things. It can remove fear. It can mend relationships. It can calm storms. It can bring about the realization of the forgiveness of sins. It can also draw groups of people together who do not normally abide together. As Ephesians 2:14 says, "He Himself is our peace, who made both groups into one and broke down the barrier of the dividing wall." I love You and thank You for this great gift. Thank You that in this name is found the unity we all long for and seek. You are the Prince of Peace who desires us to live as one in Your body and to love one another as a reflection of Your love for us.

Supplication

Jesus, I want to be known as a follower of Yours who walks in peace. When my emotional energy turns dark or disturbed, I ask that You send Your peace into my mind and spirit. Redirect my thoughts to Your Word. I want to obey Your Scripture, which says in Romans 12:18, "If possible, so far as it depends on you, be at peace with all men." Show me how to guard my emotions and thoughts so that I am in an ongoing state of peace. Help me enjoy this blessing of peace so much that others recognize it in me and desire it for themselves.

56

Rock

*All drank the same spiritual drink, for they were drinking
from a spiritual rock which followed them; and the rock
was Christ.*

1 Corinthians 10:4

Adoration

Jesus, You are the rock, the foundation on which all else is to be built. You are the source of all strength. You are the stability of all times. You are recognized by Your creation as the source. When we fail to praise You, Luke 19:40 says, "If these become silent, the stones will cry out!" The stones will cry out to the rock which made them. I praise You and worship You. I want You to receive the adoration from me that is due You. I thank You that sometimes You have let me hit rock bottom so that I would discover You are the rock at the bottom.

Confession

Jesus, Your strength and stability as the rock ought to give me comfort, assurance, security, and peace. But often I do not receive the benefits of this name of Yours because my eyes look to circumstances which seem to loom larger than You—but only because I do not keep them in perspective compared to You, the rock. I confess weariness comes upon me when I feel like the battles I face have to be fought by me. You are the rock. You are the strength of my soul. You are the victor. I confess I do not always walk in the victory You desire for me to enjoy because I forget Your name and what it means for my life.

Thanksgiving

Jesus, thank You for being the living stone from which all life has found its existence. Thank You for enduring the rejection of humanity in order that You might provide the way to draw humanity unto Yourself. As 1 Peter 2:4 says, "Coming to Him as to a living stone which has been rejected by men, but is choice and precious in the sight of God." Thank You for laying down Your life in order that I may gain mine. You are the choice and precious living stone from which I am able to freely receive the love of God. Thank You for this never-ending love.

Supplication

Jesus, make me know this name of Yours as the rock in a new and powerful way. Cause me to see Your strength in such a way that makes me marvel. I ask for You to reveal Your name to me. I know that when my faith in You is strengthened and my belief in You is as solid as a rock, I will not be disappointed. I look to the promise found in Romans 9:33, which says, "Behold, I lay in Zion a stone of stumbling and a rock of offense, and he who believes in Him will not be disappointed." Give me the full expression of this name in my life so that I can testify to Your power and strength in such a way that people will want to be saved. I ask for Your grace in this matter.

57

OUR HOPE

*Paul, an apostle of Christ Jesus according to
the commandment of God our Savior,
and of Christ Jesus, who is our hope.*

1 TIMOTHY 1:1

Adoration

Jesus, You are my hope. You are the sum total of all that is good and will be good in my life. Because of You I know I can trust that there is a perfectly designed plan You are working out for the highest good of all. I praise and worship You and this name of Yours, our hope. Without You as our hope, I cannot think of brighter days ahead or envision eternity with God. We often grieve as those who do not have hope for our loved ones. But because of You, we are able to hope. As Colossians 1:27 says, "To [His saints] God willed to make known what is the riches of the glory of this mystery among the Gentiles, which is Christ in you, the hope of glory."

Confession

Jesus, in the flesh and in my weakness, I forget that You are our hope. I forget that You have said all will be well. When I do this, my emotions become rattled and my worry increases. Forgive me for neglecting so great a hope within me, which is You—the hope of glory. You are glory. You are beauty. In Your eyes is eternal life. Help me see You, even if I can only see You as Paul wrote in 1 Corinthians 13:12: "in a mirror dimly." Give me the ability to see what I can of You while in this life so that I will be diligent to fulfill the purpose You have for me to carry out.

Thanksgiving

Thank You, Jesus, that in You I have hope. Thank You for the promises found in Scripture through which I can discover the hope of who You are. Thank You for leaving us the written Word of God which is able to teach us and instruct us according to the way we should go. I offer You my heart of gratitude for Your gift of hope. Thank You for the truth found in 2 Thessalonians 2:16-17, which says, "Now may our Lord Jesus Christ Himself and God our Father, who has loved us and given us eternal comfort and good hope by grace, comfort and strengthen your hearts in every good work and word." May I find the comfort and strength You promise in this name, our hope, so that I may continue in good works and words.

Supplication

Jesus, restore my hope in Your name. Restore my belief in glory. I ask that You remind me of this name of Yours on a regular basis. When the distractions of life set in, redirect my thoughts to You. Do not let me dwell on the distractions. When I have failed or fallen into sin, convict me toward repentance quickly so that I may find hope in this name of Yours again. Help me feel Your presence in such a way that makes this name, our hope, an ongoing reality in my life.

58

PROPHET

Jesus said to them, "A prophet is not without honor except in his hometown and among his own relatives and in his own household."

MARK 6:4

Adoration

Jesus, in fulfilling the role of prophet, You were and are the spokesperson for God. You also came as a proclaimer of the future. The prophets prior to You began their messages with the phrase, "Thus says the Lord." But when You spoke God's words, You simply said, "I say to you…" All the previous prophets were merely articulating what God had told them to tell the people. Yet when You spoke, You spoke with the authority of God because You are God, as John 1:1 reminds me. I worship You and honor You for living out this name so that we could hear from God through the perfection of Your unity with Him and Your sinless life.

Confession

Jesus, a prophet tells people to repent. A prophet speaks from the heart of God. You, as the prophet of God, have made known to me my sins for which I need to repent. I repent of my sins before You and ask that You will cleanse me from all unrighteousness according to the purification from Your shed blood on the cross. Thank You for the forgiveness that is made available to me each and every day so that I only have to come to You in repentance to receive the gift of cleansing through You, the prophet and Savior of my soul.

Thanksgiving

Thank You, Jesus, for speaking to us the very words of God. Thank You for revealing Your commandments of loving God and loving others. Thank You that You have not hidden the wisdom of the ages from us, but You have made it plain as the prophet of God. I give You all my gratitude for showing me what I need to do in order to please God. May my prayers and actions reflect Your rule in my life. May I be guided in such a way through Your prophetic words that I walk in cadence with my King and His will for my life.

Supplication

Jesus, Hebrews 1:1-2 tells us of this name of Yours when it says, "God, after He spoke long ago to the fathers in the prophets in many portions and in many ways, in these last days has spoken to us in His Son, whom He appointed heir of all things, through whom also He made the world." Through Your prophetic role, the last word on any and every subject matter is made known. You have the final say-so on everything. The problems in my life arise when I do not surrender to You, the prophet, giving You the final say in my life. I want to surrender to Your Word as the prophet always, Jesus. Help me surrender more completely to You.

59

RESURRECTION AND THE LIFE

Jesus said to her, "I am the resurrection and the life;
he who believes in Me will live even if he dies."

JOHN 11:25

Adoration

Jesus, no other name sums up Your purpose in coming to earth as much as this one. Thank You for being the resurrection and the life so that I have the pathway to God through You. Believing in You is all You ask of me in order to give me eternal life. I praise You for providing the way for me to experience the unending love of the Father through Your death, burial, and resurrection. I worship You for the totality of Your sacrifice, which You made out of love for me.

Confession

Jesus, I confess that even though I know this name of Yours, and I believe in You for salvation, I do not share this name with very many other people. Forgive me for neglecting to use the time, talents, and treasures You have given me in order to testify of You as much as I possibly can. Forgive me for forgetting my purpose, which is to tell others about You and the love You offer as the resurrection and the life.

Thanksgiving

Thank You that I do not need to fear death because You are the resurrection and the life. Thank You that I do not need to have anxiety when I consider my loved ones who have passed on and entered Your presence. You hold the keys of death, and You hold the keys of life. As it says in Revelation 1:17-18, "When I saw Him, I fell at His feet like a dead man. And He placed His right hand on me, saying, 'Do not be afraid; I am the first and the last, and the living One; and I was dead, and behold, I am alive forevermore, and I have the keys of death and of Hades.'" Thank You for Your power over death.

Supplication

Jesus, make me to be steadfast, immovable, and always abounding in Your work. I know that what I do for You and in Your name is never in vain. As the resurrection and the life, You have achieved victory over death and sin. As it is written in 1 Corinthians 15:55-58, "'O death, where is your victory? O death, where is your sting?' The sting of death is sin, and the power of sin is the law; but thanks be to God, who gives us the victory through our Lord Jesus Christ. Therefore, my beloved brethren, be steadfast, immovable, always abounding in the work of the Lord, knowing that your toil is not in vain in the Lord." I want to be fervent in how I serve You, Jesus. Give me the wisdom, strength, and empowerment to do that.

60

One Who Sets Free

If the Son makes you free, you will be free indeed.
John 8:36

Adoration

Jesus, I know that freedom is never free. It is because of Your costly gift of salvation that You can offer each of us the gift of freedom. I honor Your name as the one who sets free. I worship You for the love You showed in making freedom possible for me. I lift Your name high and hope You will enjoy my praise of who You are. I hope I will make You smile as I lift up Your name in awe of what You have done for me. Your freedom guards me. Your freedom guides me. Your freedom enables me to live out my purpose on this earth. Thank You for being the freedom I need in order to experience Your love fully and completely.

Confession

Jesus, even though I have been set free through Your gift, I am sometimes bound by sin, the flesh, or distractions. I do not want to waste another minute doing that which does not bring about good in my life or in the lives of others. I want to use the freedom You have given me in order to help others discover the gift of this freedom as well. Forgive me for neglecting to make this expression of Your name, the one who sets free, a visible part of my life and a present part of my conversations.

Thanksgiving

Jesus, thank You for freedom. Thank You for waging victorious warfare in every battle I face. I am not fighting *for* victory. Because of You, I am fighting *from* a position of victory—the victory You have already achieved as the one who sets free. I am not a prisoner of war. I am not a casualty of the battlefield. I am not a slave to my flesh or the world's ways. In You, I am fully and completely free to live out the destiny You have placed within my soul. Let me learn the lessons I have been placed here to learn. Let me teach the lessons I have been placed here to teach. Thank You that I am free to do both.

Supplication

Jesus, I ask that You help me understand what Your freedom truly is. I want to know the truth from You. Protect me from mixing in worldly wisdom or even "religious" wisdom with Your truth. Give me discernment. Enlighten my heart and mind. Bring me to a point of surrender so that I can taste the glory of Your freedom in and through me. Show me what it means to live freely, and then empower me to show others how to live according to this awareness of You, the one who sets free.

61

KINSMAN REDEEMER

My daughter, shall I not seek security for you,
that it may be well with you?
Now is not Boaz our kinsman,
with whose maids you were?
Behold, he winnows barley at
the threshing floor tonight.

RUTH 3:1-2

Adoration

Jesus, Your name as kinsman redeemer comes from the concept of a redeemer in biblical times. It arises from situations when a person lacked any ability to secure for himself or herself a future of goodness and hope, but a relative, a kinsman redeemer, stepped in to offer the security that was needed. You are humanity's kinsman redeemer, full of life-giving love and safety. Our hope rests in Your faithfulness. I praise and worship You for rescuing me from a doomed future of separation from God due to my own sinfulness.

Confession

Jesus, not only did You come to redeem me, but You came so that all who trust in You will be redeemed and receive the gift of eternal life through You. As John 3:16 says, "God so loved the world, that He gave His only begotten Son, that whoever believes in Him shall not perish, but have eternal life." It is through believing in You that we receive eternal life. Forgive me for keeping this good news to myself and not sharing with others who are in desperate need of a kinsman redeemer.

Thanksgiving

Jesus, You are blessed in all You do and say. This blessing is passed on to us when You redeem us from all that Satan seeks to entangle us in. Thank You for freeing me from the schemes of the devil. Thank You for redeeming me from hopelessness and despair. Thank You for providing me with the nourishment and finances I need to live out my days on earth. You are my source. You caused me to know You as my source when you redeemed me as the manifestation of this wonderful name, my kinsman redeemer.

Supplication

Jesus, make me to know Your ways. Create in me a heart that is drawn to You regularly and with a level of passion I didn't even know was possible. Give me a desire to know Your Word. You have redeemed me from eternal separation and torment. Use my life, which You have redeemed, to bring You joy. You say in Your Word that You desire for me to think about You and abide in You. I ask that You draw me close to You so that I can fully feel what it means to abide in Your love.

62

LORD OF GLORY

*We speak God's wisdom in a mystery, the hidden wisdom
which God predestined before the ages to our glory;
the wisdom which none of the rulers
of this age has understood;
for if they had understood it they would
not have crucified the Lord of glory.*

1 CORINTHIANS 2:7-8

Adoration

Jesus, all glory and all honor and all praise belong to You. You are the Lord of glory. You are not only glorious, but You are the highest expression of all glory. My heart sings to You with praises that my mouth is unable to form. Listen to the worship that comes from my heart, Jesus, and take delight in the love I shower upon You. As the Lord of glory, it is Your choice to whom You will reveal Your glory. Will You reveal it to me so that I can bask in this name, Lord of glory?

Confession

Jesus, I may not always realize it, but I glorify so many things other than You when I choose to give them more of my attention and thoughts than I give You. When I allow other things or people to influence my own worldview more than You, I am yielding glory to an idol instead of honoring the Lord of glory. Forgive me for how I marginalize You through focusing so heavily on distractions which keep my heart from You. These may seem like small actions or thoughts in the moment, but anything that steals Your glory is a major detriment to my spiritual walk with You. I ask for Your mercy and tender care in drawing my praise back to You.

Thanksgiving

Thank You, Jesus, for shining Your light of glory in this world. Thank You that You are the Lord of glory. If I will shift my gaze from the difficulties and challenges I experience in my life and turn it instead onto Your glory, I will receive the peace, power, and provision I need. Thank You for making it all so accessible to me through Your loving gift of glory. Your glory lights my way. Your glory defends me from darkness. Your glory brings joy to my heart. May I know Your glory more fully as You continue to reveal this name to me, Lord of glory.

Supplication

Jesus, show me how I can radiate Your glory to others. You are the Lord of glory, and I want other people to see how beautiful You are. What can I do to glorify You in my relationships? What can I do to glorify You in my work? Is there something that I can do which will bring You greater glory in my thoughts or words? I ask for wisdom on how to honor this name, Lord of glory, through my life choices. I also ask that You empower me to walk this out before You in the perfect counsel of Your will. I love You, and I pray that You will glorify Your name as I seek to advance Your kingdom agenda on earth.

63

THE LAST ADAM

It is written, "The first man, Adam, became a living soul."
The last Adam became a life-giving spirit.

1 CORINTHIANS 15:45

Adoration

Jesus, because of the sin of humanity, You had to become the creation You made in order to save us. You had to enter our world in order to undo the damage we brought on ourselves through our sin. The first Adam sinned by rejecting Your overarching rule. So You came as the last Adam, a life-giving spirit—the one who is able to save our souls from the punishment of sin. I praise and honor You for Your great love. This great love motivated You to enter the world in order to save the world from the results of our rebellion against You.

Confession

Jesus, I sometimes hold that certain sins are more damaging than others. They are what I see as the "big" sins. But Jesus, any rebellion against You is a big sin. Adam took the forbidden fruit which his wife gave him and ate it. This ushered in separation from a holy God and from the original garden filled with love, light, purity, and life.

Forgive me for my sins, Jesus. Forgive me for lying. Forgive me for not keeping my word. Forgive me for my frustrations with myself which devalue Your image in me. You came as the last Adam because You highly value me. May I value myself as You do so that I can walk in close fellowship with You all the days of this life.

Thanksgiving

Jesus, thank You for entering our realm—the realm of flesh, blood, sinew, joints, and matter—in order to live as the last Adam and provide the pathway to salvation. Thank You for Your saving grace, which You carried out in Your death on the cross. You did away with the fear and anxiety which plague us as a people. By trusting You and loving You, this fear is replaced with unending love. Thank You for Your compassion, which shows up in this name of Yours, the last Adam.

Supplication

Jesus, help me honor Your name as the last Adam by honoring and cooperating with the sanctification process in my life. Show me what I need to do in order to mature spiritually. I want to walk in the newness of life You supply. Replace judgment in my heart with compassion for others and myself. Replace jealousy with joy. I ask that Your Spirit manifest within me the purity You provide as the last Adam. Show me what I can do in order to please You.

64

THE NAME
NO ONE KNOWS

*His eyes are a flame of fire, and on His head
are many diadems; and He has a name written
on Him which no one knows except Himself.*

REVELATION 19:12

Adoration

Jesus, I praise You for Your holiness. You are truly set apart. You are beyond my understanding with the finite mind I have been given. You have made Yourself known to all of us through the many names which reveal Your attributes. Yet this name, the name no one knows, reminds us of Your holiness. It draws attention to Your greatness. It reveals Your majesty in such a way that brings awe and wonder. I worship You with all I am, knowing that my worship is but a drop in the ocean when it comes to the worship You deserve.

Confession

Jesus, there is so much about You I do not know or understand. This name of Yours that no one knows is merely a hint of all I do not know. Yet, despite my inability and inadequacy in knowing

You, You have made Yourself known to me through so many other names. Forgive me for failing to seek You regularly and honor You fully. Forgive me for not spending more time with You and abiding in You. Forgive me for questioning You when I do not understand the decisions You make or the direction in which You lead me.

Thanksgiving

Jesus, thank You for Your holiness. Thank You for Your power. Thank You for being so loving in all You are and all You feel for humanity. I praise You and worship You with my whole heart as I give You gratitude. Let what I say reflect this gratitude, not only to myself in my thoughts, but also to others in my words. Let what I do reflect the honor that this name, the name no one knows, should receive. Your ways are higher than my ways. Your thoughts are higher than my thoughts. Thank You for leading me in a manner I can understand, even if I cannot always understand You or know everything about who You are.

Supplication

Jesus, I ask You to help me live with more faith. As the existence of this name reveals, You do not always make known to me the reasons behind what goes on. Faith reveals a heart of trust within me. Give me greater faith. Give me greater trust. Give me greater boldness in taking steps of faith to follow You and know You more. Help me discern the whispering voice of the Holy Spirit so that I can please You by following You. Let me live as a kingdom steward, properly managing the time, talents, and treasures You have given me.

65

MASTER

If anyone cleanses himself from these things,
he will be a vessel for honor, sanctified,
useful to the Master,
prepared for every good work.

2 TIMOTHY 2:21

Adoration

Jesus, You are the master of all. This name speaks to Your rule and authority above all. What You command happens. What You desire comes about. You set the stars in their spots. You hung the planets where they are. You placed the moon so that it can reflect light at night and guide us. You are the master of my soul. I worship You for Your great might. I honor You for Your rule of mercy. I lift up Your name, master, as I surrender my will to Your own.

Confession

Jesus, as I go about my days, I often get distracted by my own desires. The world wants me to think that I am the master of my life. And while You have given me free will, when I choose to act as my own master, I am leaving Your will and entering into a state of chaos and sin. Forgive me for mixing Your Word with the world's words.

Forgive me for questioning Your authority as master. Give me mercy for those times that I choose sin over following You. Gossip, envy, hate, apathy toward others—these things easily appear in my heart when I am not living in surrender to You. I lay my ambitions beneath Your rule.

Thanksgiving

Thank You, Jesus, for Your attributes of control, power, strength, and might. Thank You for guiding me into Your perfect will, which leads to life. Thank You for allowing me to know You and serve You as my master. You make miracles with a single thought because You are the master over all. And You take delight in us when we recognize You as the master. I give You the gratitude of my heart as I honor You as the master who controls all. When circumstances look like they are out of control, they are simply out of *my* control. But You are the master who rules all.

Supplication

Jesus, I want to have the faith of the man at whom You marveled. Matthew 8:8-10 says, "The centurion said, 'Lord, I am not worthy for You to come under my roof, but just say the word, and my servant will be healed. For I also am a man under authority, with soldiers under me; and I say to this one, "Go!" and he goes, and to another, "Come!" and he comes, and to my slave, "Do this!" and he does it.' Now when Jesus heard this, He marveled and said to those who were following, 'Truly I say to you, I have not found such great faith with anyone in Israel.'" Give me this faith. Let me be a vehicle through which You work Your miracles because of my trust in Your name, master. You are able to do more than I could ever imagine both in and through me. Like the father in Mark 9:24, I ask for You to help my unbelief so that I can live in full faith and surrender to You.

66

KING OF THE JEWS

Where is He who has been born King of the Jews?
For we saw His star in the east and have
come to worship Him.

MATTHEW 2:2

Adoration

Jesus, the wise men searched for You when You were born on earth. They searched for the one known as the King of the Jews. This name provoked hatred and envy in King Herod because he fiercely guarded his role and his rule. But he was nothing in Your scheme. No earthly king can hold a candle to You. You are the rightful King, not only of the Jews, but of all humanity. I praise and honor You, Jesus, King of the Jews, for choosing the Jewish people as Your special possession and bringing salvation to all mankind through Your covenant and connection with them. I ask for Your blessing and favor to cover the Jews. Draw them to a saving knowledge of You, their King.

Confession

Jesus, many mocked You because of this name, King of the Jews. It is the name which was written on the sign that hung above You as You died in the flesh. In Matthew 27:37 it says, "Above His head they put up the charge against Him which read, 'THIS IS JESUS THE KING OF THE JEWS.'" They thought it was a charge, Jesus, but it was really a declaration of truth. In their arrogance, they thought they could insult You, but they were really crying out to all mankind who You truly are. I confess that I also do not honor You as King or take this role seriously in my own life as much as I should. Please forgive my self-rule and self-appointed governance.

Thanksgiving

Thank You for announcing who You are and choosing to come to earth as the King of the Jews. Thank You for Your redemptive choice of the Jewish people, through whom Your covenant of salvation is extended to all humanity. Thank You for the patience and love which You have shown Your people throughout the story of time. Thank You for Your call of Abraham so long ago, which set the Jewish people apart so that You could come through them as the King of the Jews. I love You and thank You for grafting the Gentiles into Your salvation, as Paul discusses in Romans 11.

Supplication

Jesus, burden my heart with Your heart for the Jews. Give me the love You have for Israel. Raise up within my nation a greater desire to protect and embrace Israel and the people through whom You came as the King. Bless the Jewish people, Jesus, with the awakening needed to accept You as Lord and Savior. Bless the works of their hands. Protect the borders of Israel with peace. Let the prosperity You grant to Israel testify to You as the King of the Jews. When You return to Jerusalem, Jesus, let many there be saved already through the signs and wonders You do ahead of Your return so that You will receive the welcome and love and worship due You as the King of the Jews.

67

Rabboni

Jesus said to her, "Mary!" She turned and said to Him in
Hebrew, "Rabboni!" (which means, Teacher).

John 20:16

Adoration

Jesus, You revealed Yourself to Mary when she needed You the
most. During Your time on earth, You revealed Yourself often to those
who were of a humble spirit and truly sought You. It wasn't to the wise
that You made Yourself known. It was to those who were babes and
trusted You. I adore You for Your name rabboni, meaning teacher. I
worship You for the full knowledge of all things, which is contained
in You. You hold every part of my body together, as well as all the
earth and the entire universe in which the earth resides. The sum total
of Your knowledge is beyond what our finite minds can grasp, and
yet You make Yourself available as our rabboni. You desire to teach us,
and I worship this heart of Yours, which wants us to learn.

Confession

Jesus, You have so much to teach me, and yet I waste so much of
my time thinking on other things apart from You. You are the wealth

of all knowledge, wisdom, and understanding, and yet I have the audacity to look to people to inform my life decisions. Forgive me for lacking the personal discipline to direct my thoughts to You and to reject the lies of this world. Forgive me for entertaining the deception of the enemy by what I allow into my mind. Teach me to love like You love, rabboni.

Thanksgiving

Jesus, thank You for teaching me all I know. Thank You for growing me to the level that You have. Thank You for drawing me to You so that I do not waste my life pursuing that which will burn up in heaven as wood, hay, and straw, as is talked of in 1 Corinthians 3:12-13. I am grateful for the wisdom You have revealed to me, which can direct my use of my time, talents, and treasures for work that will last. Whatever is done in the pure love of Christ will last. Thank You for revealing these things to me.

Supplication

Jesus, teach me. Rabboni, instruct me. Guide my thoughts into the fullness of the wisdom which You are willing to give me and which I am able to receive. Show me great and awesome things which I have not yet known. Open my mind to receive the illumination of the Spirit as You teach me, rabboni. Give me a hunger for Your Word, by which I can gain all I need to know for life and godliness. Teach my heart to love like Yours. Teach my spirit to show compassion to others through my thoughts and actions. Teach me how much You hate pride so that I will not entertain it within me. Teach me what is futile in life so that I don't waste my days. Teach me to number my days so that all I am is devoted to You and Your will for my life.

68

Arm of the Lord

Who has believed our message?
And to whom has the arm of
the Lord been revealed?

Isaiah 53:1

Adoration

Jesus, You are the eternal, magnificent, powerful, redeeming arm of the Lord. It is through You that victories are gained. It is through You that great works are carried out. You provide the way out of no way. You are the strength when all are weak. I praise You, arm of the Lord, for all glory is due Your great name. In Psalm 98:1 it says, "O sing to the Lord a new song, for He has done wonderful things, His right hand and His holy arm have gained the victory for Him." You have gained the victory through Your holy might, and You reveal Yourself to humanity through the power of Your miraculous arm. I sing to You a new song of glory, joy, rapturous love, and thanksgiving for this name, arm of the Lord, and what it means to me and to all of us.

Confession

Jesus, it is not hidden from us that You hate pride. Through the sin of pride we seek to lift ourselves, Your creation, to the same level as You, and that is one of the worst things we can do. It is not my arm which carries out the successes and victories in my life. It is not my arm which opens the doors of opportunity for me. It is not my arm which has gifted me in the ways that I am gifted. No, it is Your arm which has done and continues to do all these things. As Luke 1:51 says, "He has done mighty deeds with His arm; He has scattered those who were proud in the thoughts of their heart." I confess my sin of pride to You and pray that I will not be scattered because of it. Release me from the bondage of sin by the strength of Your arm.

Thanksgiving

Jesus, I glorify You and thank You for revealing Your might and the works of Your arm to us throughout all history and to me personally in my own life. As Isaiah 52:10 declares, "The LORD has bared His holy arm in the sight of all the nations, that all the ends of the earth may see the salvation of our God." Thank You for letting us see Your arm of deliverance in such a way that draws us to You in worship. Thank You for revealing the power of God in Your actions and involvement on earth. Thank You for making the arm of the Lord available to me when I need You—even in those times when I do not feel like I need You, but I really do.

Supplication

Thank You for every victory You have given me. Thank You for bringing me to this place where I am today. Jesus, it is the arm of the Lord which has brought me this far. As Psalm 44:3 says, "By their own sword they did not possess the land, and their own arm did not save them, but Your right hand and Your arm and the light of Your presence, for You favored them." Jesus, broaden my borders of influence for Your great name. Give me more land to possess which will glorify You. Favor me, Jesus, with the mighty acts of the arm of the Lord. Give me more work to do for You, more ways to direct people to You. Bless me, Jesus, through the power of the arm of the Lord in my life, and I will give You the praise and glory due You.

69

HOLY ONE OF GOD

What business do we have with each other,
Jesus of Nazareth? Have You come to destroy us?
I know who You are—the Holy One of God!

MARK 1:24

Adoration

Jesus, Your name displaces demons from their agenda. Your name drives out Satan's minions and keeps them from their attacks. Your name holds the power over death, hell, and the evil forces which wage war in this realm. Your name, holy one of God, is known and feared by every demonic force because Your name has within it the rule, authority, power, and dominion over all. I praise You for this awesome and mighty name which allows me to tap into the protection You provide.

Confession

Jesus, You are the key to my deliverance. However Satan has sought to bind me, You can set me free through this name, holy one of God. Pride, workaholism, alcoholism, overspending, narcissism, selfishness, self-righteousness—whatever the sins I am bound in, I declare that I am released by the blood of Jesus and the power of Your name, holy one of God. I confess my sins and command that the enemy have no more power over me because of Your great name, Jesus.

Thanksgiving

Thank You, Jesus, that I am not a victim of the enemy's attacks. I am a victor through Your name, holy one of God. I have all I need to live a life of freedom, joy, peace, and grace in all I do. Shower me with Your compassion so that I am not bound in shame and guilt. My heart is grateful to You for the deliverance You have given me in my past, the deliverance You are giving me in this present moment, and the deliverance You will give me when I call on Your great name, holy one of God.

Supplication

Jesus, guard me with Your blood, which empowers Your name, holy one of God. Cover me with the power of Your blood and give me a daily release from the enemy's influence over my life. Go before me, holy one of God, to make my way clear from temptation and deception. Let me walk according to the full realization of victory which Your name has given me. You are the holy one of God, and at the mention of Your name, demons must flee. Worthy are You of all praise. I give You praise, honor, and gratitude as I ask for a great manifestation of this name in my life through Your power working both in and through me to carry out Your divine will for me.

70

ETERNAL FATHER

A child will be born to us, a son will be given to us;
and the government will rest on His shoulders;
and His name will be called Wonderful Counselor,
Mighty God, Eternal Father,
Prince of Peace.

ISAIAH 9:6

Adoration

Jesus, the name Eternal Father is not commonly attributed to You in our hearts and minds. Yet this is a name You have been given because You *are* my Father—my Eternal Father. Your compassion surrounds me like the perfect love of a parent. Your nurturing love guides me as a perfect parent would. I receive Your love, Eternal Father, and trust You to make it known to me all the more throughout my days. Receive my love in return, as I am a child looking to my Eternal Father with a heart of joy, trust, and thankfulness.

Confession

Jesus, when the prophet Isaiah revealed this name of Yours in Scripture, it was because You wanted us to see that You embody more than the attributes of redemption, rule, and righteousness. You wanted us to recognize that You are a father to us in the many ways that fathers fulfill their role—in guiding, leading, giving, encouraging, and protecting those under Your care. Forgive my rebellion against you, my Eternal Father. Forgive my lack of trust in Your paternal love.

Thanksgiving

Thank You, Jesus, for revealing this name to us in Scripture; otherwise, we may never have known this character and attribute of Yours until we got to heaven. Thank You for showing us this side of You through the mention of this name. Thank You that You are a good father, one who is faithful, true, reliable, kind, caring, and loving. The love of a father is a powerful love, and You fulfill this role to the fullest. I bask in Your loving embrace, my Eternal Father. I wait in Your arms as long as I am able, not wanting to leave the security and safety Your presence provides. Thank You for meeting all my needs as a loving father does. Thank You for caring enough about me to discipline me so that I will make the right decision to repent and pursue that for which I will be grateful when I get to heaven.

Supplication

Jesus, I want to know this name of Yours more fully. I want to see Your loving eyes gazing upon me in the way a father looks on his child. Give me the heart of a child. Give me the faith of a child. Let me run into Your arms, my Eternal Father, and feel Your love. Let that love then flow through me to others as I testify of this name to those around me. You are my Eternal Father, the sum total of all I need. And You are willing to give me Your love when I look to You to receive it. Jesus, I want to know You more. I want to feel Your love. I want to love myself as You love me—not with judgment, but with compassion. Show me how to do this, my Eternal Father, as I look to You as the source of my life.

In Conclusion

There are so many names of Jesus that I had to pick only 70 for us to pray through together. But I want to leave you with a final thought regarding Jesus' many names as they show up throughout the various books of the Bible. The list below includes names and descriptive phrases that all point back to Jesus, who embodies the fullness of God Himself.

In Genesis, He is the Creator God.

In Exodus, He is the redeemer.

In Leviticus, He is your sanctification.

In Numbers, He is your guide.

In Deuteronomy, He is your teacher.

In Joshua, He is the mighty conqueror.

In Judges, He gives victory over enemies.

In Ruth, He is your kinsman, your lover, your redeemer.

In 1 Samuel, he is the root of Jesse.

In 2 Samuel, He is the Son of David.

In 1 and 2 Kings, He is King of kings and Lord of lords.

In 1 and 2 Chronicles, He is your intercessor and Great High Priest.

In Ezra, He is your temple, your house of worship.

In Nehemiah, He is your mighty wall, protecting you from your enemies.

In Esther, He stands in the gap to deliver you from your enemies.

In Job, He is the arbitrator who not only understands your struggles, but also has the power to do something about them.

In Psalms, He is your song and your reason to sing.

In Proverbs, He is your wisdom, helping you make sense of life and live it successfully.

In Ecclesiastes, He is your purpose, delivering you from vanity.

In the Song of Solomon, He is your lover, your rose of Sharon.

In Isaiah, He is the Wonderful Counselor, Mighty God, Eternal Father, and Prince of Peace. In short, He's everything you need.

In Jeremiah, He is your balm of Gilead, the soothing salve for your soul.

In Lamentations, He is the ever-faithful one upon whom you can depend.

In Ezekiel, He is the one who assures that dry, dead bones will come alive again.

In Daniel, He is the Ancient of Days, the everlasting God who never runs out of time.

In Hosea, He is your faithful lover, always beckoning you to come back—even when you have abandoned Him.

In Joel, He is your refuge, keeping you safe in times of trouble.

In Amos, He is the husbandman, the one you can depend on to stay by your side.

In Obadiah, He is Lord of the kingdom.

In Jonah, He is your salvation, bringing you back within His will.

In Micah, He is judge of the nations.

In Nahum, He is the jealous God.

In Habakkuk, He is the holy one.

In Zephaniah, He is the witness.

In Haggai, He overthrows the enemies.

In Zechariah, He is Lord of hosts.

In Malachi, He is the messenger of the covenant.

In Matthew, He is the King of the Jews.

In Mark, He is the servant.

In Luke, He is the Son of Man, feeling what you feel.

In John, He is the Son of God.

In Acts, He is the Savior of the world.

In Romans, He is the righteousness of God.

In 1 Corinthians, He is the rock that followed Israel.

In 2 Corinthians, He is the triumphant one, giving victory.

In Galatians, He is your liberty; He sets you free.

In Ephesians, He is head of the church.

In Philippians, He is your joy.

In Colossians, He is your completeness.

In 1 Thessalonians, He is your hope.

In 2 Thessalonians, He is your glory.

In 1 Timothy, He is your faith.

In 2 Timothy, He is your stability.

In Titus, He is God your Savior.

In Philemon, He is your benefactor.

In Hebrews, He is your perfection.

In James, He is the power behind your faith.

In 1 Peter, He is your example.

In 2 Peter, He is your purity.

In 1 John, He is your life.

In 2 John, He is your pattern.

In 3 John, He is your motivation.

In Jude, He is the foundation of your faith.

In Revelation, He is your coming King.

There's something awesome about the name Jesus. So make sure you wear the name through your public identification with Him, then bear the name by being willing to suffer because of your association with Him, and finally share the name as you witness to others about your Savior.

Acknowledgments

I want to thank my friends at Harvest House Publishers for their long-standing partnership in bringing my thoughts, studies, and words to print. I particularly want to thank Bob Hawkins for his friendship over the years, as well as his pursuit of excellence in leading his company. My gratitude belongs to Sherrie Slopianka, Terry Glaspey, Betty Fletcher, and Amber Holcomb. In addition, I want to thank Heather Hair for her skills and insights in collaboration on this manuscript.

THE URBAN ALTERNATIVE

The Urban Alternative (TUA) equips, empowers, and unites Christians to impact *individuals, families, churches,* and *communities* through a thoroughly kingdom agenda worldview. In teaching truth, we seek to transform lives.

The core cause of the problems we face in our personal lives, homes, churches, and societies is a spiritual one; therefore, the only way to address it is spiritually. We've tried a political, social, economic, and even a religious agenda.

It's time for a **Kingdom agenda**.

The Kingdom agenda can be defined as the visible manifestation of the comprehensive rule of God over every area of life.

The unifying central theme throughout the Bible is the glory of God and the advancement of His kingdom. The conjoining thread from Genesis to Revelation—from beginning to end—is focused on one thing: God's glory through advancing God's kingdom.

When you do not have that theme, the Bible becomes disconnected stories that are great for inspiration but seem to be unrelated in purpose and direction. The Bible exists to share God's movement in history toward the establishment and expansion of His kingdom highlighting the connectivity throughout which is the kingdom. Understanding that increases the relevancy of this several thousand-year-old manuscript to your day-to-day living, because the kingdom is not only then, it is now.

The absence of the kingdom's influence in our personal and family lives, churches, and communities has led to a deterioration in our world of immense proportions:

- People live segmented, compartmentalized lives because they lack God's kingdom worldview.
- Families disintegrate because they exist for their own satisfaction rather than for the kingdom.
- Churches are limited in the scope of their impact because they fail to comprehend that the goal of the church is not the church itself, but the kingdom.
- Communities have nowhere to turn to find real solutions for real people who have real problems because the church has become divided, in-grown, and unable to transform the cultural landscape in any relevant way.

The kingdom agenda offers us a way to see and live life with a solid hope by optimizing the solutions of heaven. When God, and His rule, is no longer the final and authoritative standard under which all else falls, order and hope leaves with Him. But the reverse of that is true as well: As long as you have God, you have hope. If God is still in the picture, and as long as His agenda is still on the table, it's not over.

Even if relationships collapse, God will sustain you. Even if finances dwindle, God will keep you. Even if dreams die, God will revive you. As long as God, and His rule, is still the overarching rule in your life, family, church, and community, there is always hope.

Our world needs the King's agenda. Our churches need the King's agenda. Our families need the King's agenda.

In many major cities, there is a loop that drivers can take when they want to get somewhere on the other side of the city, but don't necessarily want to head straight through downtown. This loop will take you close enough to the city so that you can see its towering buildings and skyline, but not close enough to actually experience it.

This is precisely what we, as a culture, have done with God. We have put Him on the "loop" of our personal, family, church, and community lives. He's close enough to be at hand should we need Him in an emergency, but far enough away that He can't be the center of who we are.

We want God on the "loop," not the King of the Bible who comes downtown into the very heart of our ways. Leaving God on the "loop" brings about dire consequences as we have seen in our own lives and with others. But when we make God, and His rule, the centerpiece of all we think, do, or say, it is then that we will experience Him in the way He longs to be experienced by us.

He wants us to be kingdom people with kingdom minds set on fulfilling His kingdom's purposes. He wants us to pray, as Jesus did, "Not my will, but Thy will be done." Because His is the kingdom, the power, and the glory.

There is only one God, and we are not Him. As King and Creator, God calls the shots. It is only when we align ourselves underneath His comprehensive hand that we will access His full power and authority in all spheres of life: personal, familial, church, and community.

As we learn how to govern ourselves under God, we then transform the institutions of family, church, and society from a biblically based kingdom worldview.

Under Him, we touch heaven and change earth.

To achieve our goal, we use a variety of strategies, approaches, and resources for reaching and equipping as many people as possible.

Broadcast Media

Millions of individuals experience *The Alternative with Dr. Tony Evans* through the daily radio broadcast playing on nearly

1,400 RADIO outlets and in over **130 countries**. The broadcast can also be seen on several television networks, and is viewable online at TonyEvans.org. You can also listen or view the daily broadcast by downloading the Tony Evans app for free in the App store. Over 10,000,000 message downloads/streams occur each year.

Leadership Training

The Tony Evans Training Center (TETC) facilitates educational programming that embodies the ministry philosophy of Dr. Tony Evans as expressed through the kingdom agenda. The training courses focus on leadership development and discipleship in the following five tracks:

- Bible and Theology
- Personal Growth
- Family and Relationships
- Church Health and Leadership Development
- Society and Community Impact Strategies

The TETC program includes courses for both local and online students. Furthermore, TETC programming includes course work for non-student attendees. Pastors, Christian leaders, and Christian laity, both local and at a distance, can seek out The Kingdom Agenda Certificate for personal, spiritual, and professional development. Some courses are valued for CEU credit as well as viable in transferring for college credit with our partner school(s). For more information, visit: tonyevanstraining.org

The Kingdom Agenda Pastors (KAP) provides a *viable network* for *like-minded pastors* who embrace the Kingdom agenda philosophy. Pastors have the opportunity to go deeper with Dr. Tony Evans as they are given greater biblical knowledge, practical applications, and resources to impact individuals, families, churches, and communities. KAP welcomes *senior and associate pastors* of all churches. KAP also offers an annual Summit held each year in Dallas with intensive seminars, workshops, and resources.

Pastors' Wives Ministry, founded by Dr. Lois Evans, provides *counsel, encouragement,* and *spiritual resources* for pastors' wives as they serve with their husbands in the ministry. A primary focus of the ministry is the KAP Summit that offers senior pastors' wives a safe place to *reflect, renew,* and *relax* along with training in personal development, spiritual growth, and care for their emotional and physical well-being.

Community & Cultural Influence

National Church Adopt-A-School Initiative (NCAASI) prepares churches across the country to impact communities by using *public schools as the primary vehicle for effecting positive social change* in urban youth and families. Leaders of churches, school districts, faith-based organizations, and other nonprofit organizations are equipped with the knowledge and tools to *forge partnerships* and build *strong social service delivery systems.* This training is based on the comprehensive church-based community impact strategy conducted by Oak Cliff Bible Fellowship. It addresses such areas as economic development, education, housing, health revitalization, family renewal, and racial reconciliation. We assist churches in tailoring the model to meet specific needs of their communities while simultaneously addressing the spiritual and moral frame of reference. Training events are held annually in the Dallas area at Oak Cliff Bible Fellowship.

Athlete's Impact (AI) exists as an outreach both into and through the sports arena. Coaches are the most influential factor in young people's lives, even ahead of their parents. With the growing rise of fatherlessness in our culture, more young people are looking to their coaches for guidance, character development, practical needs, and hope. After coaches on the influencer scale fall athletes. Athletes (whether professional or amateur) influence younger athletes and kids within their spheres of impact. Knowing this, we have made it our aim to equip and train coaches and athletes on how to live out and utilize their God-given roles for the benefit of the kingdom. We aim to do this through our iCoach App as well as resources such as *The Playbook: A Life Strategy Guide for Athletes.*

Tony Evans Films ushers in positive life change through compelling video-shorts, animation, and feature-length films. We seek to build kingdom disciples through the power of story. We use a variety of platforms for viewer consumption and have over 35,000,000 digital views. We also merge video-shorts and film with relevant Bible study materials to bring people to the saving knowledge of Jesus Christ and to strengthen the body of Christ worldwide. Tony Evans Films released our first feature-length film, *Kingdom Men Rising*, in April 2019, in over 800 theaters nationwide, in partnership with Lifeway Films.

Resource Development

We are fostering lifelong learning partnerships with the people we serve by providing a variety of published materials. Dr. Evans has published more than 100 unique titles based on over 40 years of preaching whether that is in booklet, book, or Bible study format. He also holds the honor of writing and publishing the first full-Bible commentary and study Bible by an African-American, released in 2019.

For more information, and a complimentary copy
of Dr. Evans' devotional newsletter,
call (800) 800-3222
or write TUA at P.O. Box 4000, Dallas TX 75208,
or visit us online:
www.TonyEvans.org

Tony Evans
THE URBAN ALTERNATIVE

YOUR *Eternity* IS OUR *Priority*

At The Urban Alternative, eternity is our priority—for the individual, the family, the church and the nation. The 45-year teaching ministry of Tony Evans has allowed us to reach a world in need with:

The Alternative – Our flagship radio program brings hope and comfort to an audience of millions on over 1,300 radio outlets across the country.

tonyevans.org – Our library of teaching resources provides solid Bible teaching through the inspirational books and sermons of Tony Evans.

Tony Evans Training Center – Experience the adventure of God's Word with our online classroom, providing at-your-own-pace courses for your PC or mobile device.

Tony Evans app – Packed with audio and video clips, devotionals, Scripture readings and dozens of other tools, the mobile app provides inspiration on-the-go.

Explore God's kingdom today.
Live for more than the moment.
Live for *eternity*.

tonyevans.org

Life is busy,
but Bible study is still possible.

*Subscription model

a **portable**
seminary

Explore the kingdom.
Anytime, anywhere.

TONY EVANS
TRAINING CENTER

tonyevanstraining.or